MANAGE YOUR DAY-TO-DAY

—

amazonpublishing

MANAGE

YOUR

DAY-TO-DAY

*Build Your Routine, Find Your Focus,
and Sharpen Your Creative Mind*

—

Edited by Jocelyn K. Glei
Foreword by Scott Belsky

Published by Amazon Publishing
PO Box 400818
Las Vegas, NV 89140

ISBN-13: 9781477800676
ISBN-10: 1477800670

For the creators

WHAT IS 99U?

—

For too long, the creative world has focused on idea generation at the expense of idea execution. As the legendary inventor Thomas Edison famously said, "Genius is 1 percent inspiration, and 99 percent perspiration." To make great ideas a reality, we must act, experiment, fail, adapt, and learn on a daily basis.

99U is Behance's effort to provide this "missing curriculum" for making ideas happen. Through our Webby Award–winning website, popular events, and bestselling books, we share pragmatic, action-oriented insights from leading researchers and visionary creatives.

At 99U, we don't want to give you more ideas—we want to empower you to make good on the ones you've got.

PREFACE

—

The world we work in today is not the world of Michelangelo, of Marie Curie, of Ernest Hemingway, or even of Paul Rand. It is a new world, empowered and entranced by the rapid-fire introduction of new technologies—a world where our metaphysical front door is always open, where anyone can whisper in our ear, where a "room of one's own" no longer means you're all alone.

Creative minds are exceedingly sensitive to the buzz and whir of the world around them, and we now have to contend with a constant stream of chirps, pings, and alerts at all hours of the day. As these urgent demands tug us this way and that, it becomes increasingly difficult to find a centered space for creativity.

Taking stock of this challenging new landscape, 99U's *Manage Your Day-to-Day* assembles insights around four key skill sets you must master to succeed: building a rock-solid daily routine, taming your tools (before they tame you), finding focus in a distracted world, and sharpening your creative mind.

Dedicating a chapter to each of these focus areas, we invited a group of seasoned thought leaders and creatives—Seth Godin, Stefan Sagmeister, Tony Schwartz, Gretchen Rubin, Dan Ariely, Linda Stone, Steven Pressfield, and others—to share their expertise. Our goal was to come at the problems and struggles of this new world of work from as many angles as possible.

Because we each have a unique set of strengths, weaknesses, and sensitivities, it is impossible to prescribe a single approach that will work for everyone. The right solution for you will always be personal—an idiosyncratic combination of strategies based on your own work demands, habits, and preferences.

So rather than lay out a one-size-fits-all productivity system, we provide a playbook of best practices for producing great work. Our hope is that these insights, taken together, will help you shift your mind-set, recalibrate your workflow, and push more incredible ideas to completion.

— *JOCELYN K. GLEI, editor-in-chief, 99U*

TABLE
OF
CONTENTS
–

FINDING FOCUS IN A DISTRACTED WORLD

TAMING YOUR TOOLS

SHARPENING YOUR CREATIVE MIND

Coda: A CALL TO ACTION

RETOOLING FOR A NEW ERA OF WORK

—

Scott Belsky, Founder of Behance &
author of Making Ideas Happen

Prepare for a highly concentrated dose of insights that will prove both enlightening and uncomfortable. This was my own experience, at least. My review of the early manuscript for *Manage Your Day-to-Day* raised some glaring concerns in my own mind about my productivity and mindfulness.

These new perspectives caught me off-guard—I realized that much of my most valuable energy had been unknowingly consumed by bad habits. My day-to-day practices had devolved to a point where I was at the mercy of everything around me—everything but my goals and true preferences.

It was clear that I was long overdue for a self-audit of how I manage my time in a rapidly changing work environment. So much has shifted in just the last few years: My calendar and documents are now all in the cloud. I have more devices, apps, alerts, and utilities than ever before. And with the new ability to work anywhere, the outcome of the work I do has unintentionally changed. Meanwhile, I've been out there in the thick of it, working hard but never taking stock. If you keep playing without any time-outs, your game starts to slip.

Of course, every great leader must face his or her demons in order to overcome them. I've always known this, but I wasn't aware of any immediate problems. But these days the demons are more insidious; they're the everyday annoyances, the little things that suck away our potential to do big things.

OWN THE PROBLEM

I've spent much of my career promoting strong business practices in the creative industry. Throughout my travels for Behance and in researching my book, *Making Ideas Happen*, I have spoken with countless creative people and teams about their projects and careers. With designers, writers, and entrepreneurs of all kinds, I have tried to advocate for the roll-up-your-sleeves productivity and management skills required to push ideas to fruition. My mantra has always been, "It's not about ideas, it's about making ideas happen."

Frequently I am asked to speak at conferences and companies about "creativity." I always respond with the preliminary question, "Do you have ideas?" The answer is almost always "Yes, but…"

followed by a series of obstacles like: "We work in a big company and it's hard to pursue new ideas," "We get overwhelmed with the day-to-day stuff and struggle to make progress on new stuff," or "Our leadership asks for innovation but keeps getting in the way."

Alas, when folks want to talk creativity, what they're really seeking is help with execution, ways to take action more effectively. Once the true problem becomes clear, the blame quickly shifts to the ecosystem. The company is either too big or too small. The management is screwing things up. Or it's the "process" that gets in the way.

It's time to stop blaming our surroundings and start taking responsibility. While no workplace is perfect, it turns out that our gravest challenges are a lot more primal and personal. Our individual practices ultimately determine what we do and how well we do it. Specifically, it's our routine (or lack thereof), our capacity to work proactively rather than reactively, and our ability to systematically optimize our work habits over time that determine our ability to make ideas happen.

DON'T JUST DO, RETOOL YOUR DOING

Often I'll ask a great team about the last time they had a meeting to discuss how they work. Aside from the occasional mention of an annual off-site, I usually get a null response. Why? Everyone's too busy doing stuff to take a pause and make some changes to *how* they do stuff. I've never seen a team sport without a huddle, yet we'll continue working for months—if not years—with clients and colleagues without ever taking a step back, taking stock, and making improvements to our systems.

As individuals we're even worse off; we never have off-sites with ourselves. Seldom do we stop doing what we're doing to think about (and rework) how we're doing it. The biggest problem with any routine is that you do it without realizing it. Bad habits creep in, especially as we naturally acclimate to a changing work environment, and we end up working at the mercy of our surroundings.

THE ERA OF REACTIONARY WORKFLOW

The biggest problem we face today is "reactionary workflow." We have started to live a life pecking away at the many inboxes around us, trying to stay afloat by responding and reacting to the latest thing: e-mails, text messages, tweets, and so on.

Through our constant connectivity to each other, we have become increasingly reactive to what comes to us rather than being proactive about what matters most to us. Being informed and connected becomes a disadvantage when the deluge supplants your space to think and act.

As you'll see in the discussions ahead, the shortcuts and modern marvels of work don't come without a cost. Thriving in the new era of work requires us to question the norms and so-called efficiencies that have edged their way into our day-to-day.

TIME TO OPTIMIZE

We need to rethink our workflow from the ground up.

Paradoxically, you hold both the problem and the solution to your day-to-day challenges. No matter where you work or what horrible top-down systems plague your work, your mind and energy are yours and yours alone. You can surrender your day-to-day and the potential of your work to the burdens that surround you. Or, you can audit the way you work and own the responsibility of fixing it.

This book offers many deep and powerful insights into optimizing your day-to-day rhythms. You'll likely find that your work habits have drifted to accommodate your surroundings rather than to meet your preferences. Use this book as an opportunity to reassess. Take a rare pause from your incessant doing to rethink *how* you do what you do.

Only by taking charge of your day-to-day can you truly make an impact in what matters most to you. I urge you to build a better routine by stepping outside of it, find your focus by rising above the constant cacophony, and sharpen your creative prowess by analyzing what really matters most when it comes to making your ideas happen.

–

CHAPTER ONE

BUILDING A ROCK-SOLID ROUTINE

–

How to give structure, rhythm, and purpose to your daily work

Woody Allen once said that 80 percent of success is showing up. Having written and directed fifty films in almost as many years, Allen clearly knows something about accomplishment. How, when, and where you show up is the single most important factor in executing on your ideas.

That's why so many creative visionaries stick to a daily routine. Choreographer Twyla Tharp gets up at the crack of dawn every day and hails a cab to go to the gym—a ritual she calls her "trigger moment." Painter Ross Bleckner reads the paper, meditates, and then gets to the studio by 8 a.m. so that he can work in the calm quiet of the early morning. Writer Ernest Hemingway wrote five hundred words a day, come hell or high water.

Truly great creative achievements require hundreds, if not thousands, of hours of work, and we have to make time every single day to put in those hours. Routines help us do this by setting expectations about availability, aligning our workflow with our energy levels, and getting our minds into a regular rhythm of creating.

At the end of the day—or, really, from the beginning—building a routine is all about persistence and consistency. Don't wait for inspiration; create a framework for it.

LAYING THE GROUNDWORK FOR AN EFFECTIVE ROUTINE

—

Mark McGuinness

If you want to create something worthwhile with your life, you need to draw a line between the world's demands and your own ambitions. Yes, we all have bills to pay and obligations to satisfy. But for most of us there's a wide gray area between the have-tos and want-tos in our lives. If you're not careful, that area will fill up with e-mail, meetings, and the requests of others, leaving no room for the work *you* consider important.

A great novel, a stunning design, a game-changing piece of software, a revolutionary company—achievements like these take time, thought, craft, and persistence. And on any given day, this effort will never appear as urgent as those four e-mails (in the last half hour) from Client X or Colleague Y asking for something that can likely wait a few hours, if not days.

No one likes the feeling that other people are waiting—impatiently—for a response. At the beginning of the day, faced with an overflowing inbox, an array of voice mail messages, and the list of next steps from your last meeting, it's tempting to "clear the decks" before starting your own work. When you're up-to-date, you tell yourself, it will be easier to focus.

The trouble with this approach is it means spending the best part of the day on *other people's priorities*. By the time you settle down to your own work, it could be mid-afternoon, when your energy dips and your brain slows.

"Oh well, maybe tomorrow will be better," you tell yourself.

But tomorrow brings another pile of e-mails, phone messages, and to-do list items. If you carry on like this, you will spend most of your time on reactive work, responding to incoming demands and answering questions framed by other people. And you will never create anything truly worthwhile.

CREATIVE WORK FIRST, REACTIVE WORK SECOND

The single most important change you can make in your working habits is to switch to creative work first, reactive work second. This means blocking off a large chunk of time every day for creative work on your own priorities, with the phone and e-mail off.

I used to be a frustrated writer. Making this switch turned me into a productive writer. Now, I start the working day with several hours of writing. I never schedule meetings in the morning, if I can avoid it. So whatever else happens, I always get my most important work done—and looking back, all of my biggest successes have been the result of making this simple change.

Yet there wasn't a single day when I sat down to write an article, blog post, or book chapter without a string of people waiting for me to get back to them.

It wasn't easy, and it still isn't, particularly when I get phone messages beginning "I sent you an e-mail *two hours ago*...!"

By definition, this approach goes against the grain of others' expectations and the pressures they put on you. It takes willpower to switch off the world, even for an hour. It feels uncomfortable, and sometimes people get upset. But it's better to disappoint a few people over small things, than to surrender your dreams for an empty inbox. Otherwise you're sacrificing your potential for the illusion of professionalism.

THE BUILDING BLOCKS OF A GREAT DAILY ROUTINE

Of course, it's all well and good to say buckle down and ignore pesky requests, but how can you do so on a daily basis?

Start with the rhythm of your energy levels. Certain times of day are especially conducive to focused creativity, thanks to circadian rhythms of arousal and mental alertness. Notice when you seem to have the most energy during the day, and dedicate those valuable periods to your most important creative work. Never book a meeting during this time if you can help it. And don't waste any of it on administrative work!

Use creative triggers. Stick to the same tools, the same surroundings, even the same background music, so that they become associative triggers for you to enter your creative zone. Here's how it works for Stephen King:

> *There are certain things I do if I sit down to write. I have a glass of water or a cup of tea. There's a certain time I sit down, from 8:00 to 8:30, somewhere within that half hour every morning. I have my vitamin pill and my music, sit in the same seat, and the papers are all arranged in the same places. The cumulative purpose of doing these things the same way every day seems to be a way of saying to the mind, you're going to be dreaming soon.[1]*

Manage to-do list creep. Limit your daily to-do list. A 3″ × 3″ Post-it is perfect—if you can't fit everything on a list that size, how will you do it all in one day? If you keep adding to your to-do list during the day, you will never finish—and your motivation will plummet. Most things can wait till tomorrow. So let them.

Capture every commitment. Train yourself to record every commitment you make (to yourself or others) somewhere that will make it impossible to forget. This will help you respond to requests more efficiently and make you a better collaborator. More important, it will give you peace of mind—when you are confident that everything has been captured reliably, you can focus on the task at hand.

Establish hard edges in your day. Set a start time and a finish time for your workday—even if you work alone. Dedicate different times of day to different activities: creative work, meetings, correspondence, administrative work, and so on. These hard edges keep tasks from taking longer than they need to and encroaching on your other important work. They also help you avoid workaholism, which is far less productive than it looks.

~∞~

A truly effective routine is always personal—a snug fit with your own talent and inclinations. So experiment with these building blocks and notice which combination gives you the best foundation for doing your best work. You'll know it's effective when your daily schedule starts to feel less like a mundane routine and more like a creative ritual.

MARK MCGUINNESS is a London-based coach for creative professionals. He works with clients all over the world and consults for creative companies. He is the author of Resilience: Facing Down Rejection and Criticism on the Road to Success *and a columnist for 99U.*

→ www.LateralAction.com

"I don't wait for moods. You accomplish nothing if you do that. Your mind must know it has got to get down to work."

— PEARL S. BUCK

HARNESSING THE POWER OF FREQUENCY

—

Gretchen Rubin

We tend to overestimate what we can do in a short period, and underestimate what we can do over a long period, provided we work slowly and consistently. Anthony Trollope, the nineteenth-century writer who managed to be a prolific novelist while also revolutionizing the British postal system, observed, "A small daily task, if it be really daily, will beat the labours of a spasmodic Hercules." Over the long run, the unglamorous habit of frequency fosters both productivity and creativity.

As a writer, I work every single day, including weekends, holidays, and vacations. Usually I write for many hours during a day, though sometimes it might be a stint as short as fifteen minutes—and I never skip a day. I've found that this kind of frequent work makes it possible to accomplish more, with greater originality, for several reasons.

Frequency makes starting easier. Getting started is always a challenge. It's hard to start a project from scratch, and it's also hard each time you re-enter a project after a break. By working every day, you keep your momentum going. You never have time to feel detached from the process. You never forget your place, and you never need to waste time reviewing your work to get back up to speed or reminding yourself what you've already done. Because your project is fresh in your mind, it's easy to pick up where you left off.

Frequency keeps ideas fresh. You're much more likely to spot surprising relationships and to see fresh connections among ideas, if your mind is constantly humming with issues related to your work. When I'm deep in a project, everything I experience seems to relate to it in a way that's absolutely exhilarating. The entire world becomes more interesting. That's critical, because I have a voracious need for material, and as I become hyperaware of potential fodder, ideas pour in. By contrast, working sporadically makes it hard to keep your focus. It's easy to become blocked, confused, or distracted, or to forget what you were aiming to accomplish.

Frequency keeps the pressure off. If you're producing just one page, one blog post, or one sketch a week, you expect it to be pretty darned good, and you start to fret about quality. I knew a writer who could hardly bring herself to write. When she did manage to keep herself in front of her laptop for a spate of work, she felt enormous pressure to be brilliant; she evaluated the product of each work session with an uneasy and highly critical eye. She hadn't done much work, so what she did accomplish had to be extraordinarily good. Because I write every day, no one day's work seems particularly important. I have good days and I have bad days. Some days, I don't get much done at all. But that's okay, because I know I'm working steadily. My consequent lack of anxiety puts me in a more playful frame of mind and allows me to experiment and take risks. If something doesn't work out, I have plenty of time to try a different approach.

Frequency sparks creativity. You might be thinking, "Having to work frequently, whether or not I feel inspired, will force me to lower my standards." In my experience, the effect is just the opposite. Often folks achieve their best work by grinding out the product. Creativity arises from a constant churn of ideas, and one of the easiest ways to encourage that fertile froth is to keep your mind engaged with your project. When you work regularly, inspiration strikes regularly.

Frequency nurtures frequency. If you develop the habit of working frequently, it becomes much easier to sit down and get something done even when you don't have a big block of time; you don't have to take time to acclimate yourself. I know a writer married to a painter, and she told me, "We talk about the 'ten-minute rule.' If our work is going well, we can sit down and get something good done in ten minutes." Frequency allows us to make use of these short windows of time. On a related note…

Frequency fosters productivity. It's no surprise that you're likely to get more accomplished if you work daily. The very fact of each day's accomplishment helps the next day's work come more smoothly and pleasantly. Nothing is more satisfying that seeing yourself move steadily toward a big goal. Step by step, you make your way forward. That's why practices such as daily writing exercises or keeping a daily blog can be so helpful. You see yourself do the work, which shows you that you can do the work. Progress is reassuring and inspiring; panic and then despair set in when you find yourself getting nothing done day after day. One of the painful ironies of work life is that the anxiety of procrastination often makes people even less likely to buckle down in the future.

Frequency is a realistic approach. Frequency is helpful when you're working on a creative project on the side, with pressing obligations from a job or your family. Instead of feeling perpetually frustrated that you don't have any time for your project, you *make* yourself make time, every day. If you do a little bit each day, you can get a lot done over the course of months and years (see above). Also, it's true that frequency doesn't have to be a daily frequency; what's most important is consistency. The more widely spaced your work times, however, the less you reap all of these benefits.

The opposite of a profound truth is usually also true. While there are many advantages to frequency over the long term, sometimes it's fun to take a boot camp approach, to work very intensely for a very short period of time. In *Making Comics*, Scott McCloud recommends what he calls the 24-hour comic: "Draw an entire 24-page comic book in a single 24-hour period. No script. No preparation. Once the clock starts ticking, it doesn't stop until you're done. Great shock therapy for the creatively blocked." I love plugging along in my work bit by bit, but occasionally it's even more useful to take a big, ambitious step. By tackling more instead of less, I enjoy a surge of energy and focus.

I have a long list of "Secrets of Adulthood," the lessons I've learned as I've grown up, such as: "It's the task that's never started that's more tiresome," "The days are long, but the years are short," and "Always leave plenty of room in the suitcase." One of my most helpful Secrets is, "What I do every day matters more than what I do once in a while."

Day by day, we build our lives, and day by day, we can take steps toward making real the magnificent creations of our imaginations.

GRETCHEN RUBIN *is the author of the bestsellers*
Happier at Home *and* The Happiness Project—*accounts of her experiences test-driving ancient wisdom, scientific studies, and lessons from popular culture about happiness. On her blog, she reports on her daily adventures in happiness.*

→ www.happiness-project.com

"We are what we repeatedly do. Excellence, then, is not an act, but a habit."

— ARISTOTLE

Q&A:

HONING YOUR
CREATIVE PRACTICE

—

with Seth Godin

Seth Godin knows a few things about getting stuff done. He has consistently innovated as an entrepreneur, a writer, and an educator—all the while producing an incredible body of work that includes numerous groundbreaking ventures such as the Domino Project, Squidoo, and the first "Alternative MBA Program," not to mention fourteen bestselling books. We chatted with him about how cultivating a daily practice is a necessary prerequisite to achieving great things.

What's the hardest part about getting a daily routine right?

Everybody who does creative work has figured out how to deal with their own demons to get their work done. There is no evidence that setting up your easel like Van Gogh makes you paint better. Tactics are idiosyncratic. But strategies are universal, and there are a lot of talented folks who are not succeeding the way they want to because their strategies are broken.

The strategy is simple, I think. The strategy is to have a practice, and what it means to have a practice is to regularly and reliably do the work in a habitual way.

There are many ways you can signify to yourself that you are doing your practice. For example, some people wear a white lab coat or a particular pair of glasses, or always work in a specific place—in doing these things, they are professionalizing their art.

The notion that I do my work here, now, like this, even when I do not feel like it, and *especially* when I do not feel like it, is very important. Because lots and lots of people are creative when they feel like it, but you are only going to become a professional if you do it when you don't feel like it. And that emotional waiver is why this is your work and not your hobby.

What do people struggle with the most, outside of the hard work of a daily routine?

The practice is a big part. The second part of it, which I think is really critical, is understanding that being creative means that you have to sell your ideas. If you're a professional, you do not get to say, "Ugh, now I have to go sell it"—selling it is part of it because if you do not sell it, there is no art. No fair embracing one while doing a sloppy job on the other.

Can you think of any artists who did not possess that sales ability originally but were able to cultivate it?

I've never met anybody who is great at selling who was born that way. I think that all the people who have figured out how to do this for a living have figured it out because it was important to them, not because it came naturally. Whereas I know tons of people who call themselves artists who were born with talents and never really had to push themselves to be good at it. They think they are entitled to make a living at this thing, but they are not willing to do the hard part—selling—that everyone finds hard.

Sometimes we work hard in the short term but still fail to achieve our big-picture goals. How do you keep your short-term work aligned with your long-term objectives?

The reason you might be having trouble with your practice in the long run—if you were capable of building a practice in the short run—is nearly always because you are afraid. The fear, the resistance, is very insidious. It doesn't leave a lot of fingerprints, but the person who manages to make a movie short that blows everyone away but can't raise enough cash to make a feature film, the person who gets a little freelance work here and there but can't figure out how to turn it into a full-time gig—that person is practicing self-sabotage.

These people sabotage themselves because the alternative is to put themselves into the world as someone who knows what they are doing. They are afraid that if they do that, they will be seen as a fraud. It's incredibly difficult to stand up at a board meeting or a conference or just in front of your peers and say, "I know how to do this. Here is my work. It took me a year. It's great."

This is hard to do for two reasons: (1) it opens you to criticism, and (2) it puts you into the world as someone who knows what you are doing, which means tomorrow you also have to know what you are doing, and you have just signed up for a lifetime of knowing what you are doing.

It's much easier to whine and sabotage yourself and blame the client, the system, and the economy. This is what you hide from—the noise in your head that says you are not good enough, that says it is not perfect, that says it could have been better.

SETH GODIN has written fourteen books that have been translated into more than thirty languages. Every one has been a bestseller. He writes about the post-industrial revolution, the way ideas spread, marketing, quitting, leadership, and, most of all, changing everything.

→ www.sethgodin.com

"You can't TRY to do things,

you must simply DO them."

— RAY BRADBURY

BUILDING RENEWAL INTO YOUR WORKDAY

—

Tony Schwartz

Zeke is a creative director at a large agency. The workday he described when we first met was typical of the managers and leaders I meet in my travels.

After six or six and a half hours of sleep—which never felt like enough—Zeke's alarm went off at 5:30 a.m. each morning. His first move was to take his iPhone off the night table and check his e-mail. He told himself he did this in case something urgent had come in overnight, but the truth was he just couldn't resist.

Zeke tried to get to the gym at least two times a week, but he traveled frequently, and at home he was often just too tired to work out.

Once he got to work—around 7:30 a.m. most days—Zeke grabbed a cup of coffee, sat down at his desk, and checked his e-mail again. By then, twenty-five or more new messages were typically waiting in his in-box. If he didn't have an early meeting, he might be online for an hour or more without once looking up.

Zeke's days were mostly about meetings. They were usually scheduled one after the other with no time in between. As a result, he would race off to the next meeting without digesting what he'd just taken in at the last one.

Lunch was something Zeke squeezed in. He usually brought food back to his desk from the cafeteria and worked while he ate. Around two or three in the afternoon, depending on how much sleep he'd gotten the previous night, Zeke began to feel himself fading. Given his company's culture, taking even a short nap wasn't an option. Instead, for a quick hit of energy, he found himself succumbing to a piece of someone's leftover birthday cake, or running to the vending machine for a Snickers bar.

With so many urgent demands, Zeke tended to put off any intensive, challenging work for later. By the end of the day, however, he rarely had the energy to get to it. Even so, he found it difficult to leave work with so much unfinished business. By the time he finally did, usually around 7:30 or 8 p.m., he was pretty much running on empty.

After dinner, Zeke tried to get to some of the work he had put off earlier in the day. Much of the time, he simply ended up returning to e-mail or playing games online. Either way, he typically stayed up later than he knew he should.

How closely does this match your experience? To the extent that it does resonate, how did this happen? Most important, can you imagine working the way you do now for the next ten or twenty years?

YOUR CAPACITY IS LIMITED

The challenge is that the demand in our lives increasingly exceeds our capacity. Think of capacity as the fuel that makes it possible to bring your skill and talent fully to life. Most of us take our capacity for granted, because for most of our lives we've had enough.

What's changed is that between digital technology and rising complexity, there's more information and more requests coming at us, faster and more relentlessly than ever.

Unlike computers, however, human beings aren't meant to operate continuously, at high speeds, for long periods of time. Rather, we're designed to move rhythmically between spending and renewing our energy. Our brains wave between high and low electrical frequencies. Our hearts beat at varying intervals. Our lungs expand and contract depending on demand. It's not sufficient to be good at inhaling. Indeed, the more deeply you exhale, the calmer and more capable you become.

Instead, we live linear lives, progressively burning down our energy reservoirs throughout the day. It's the equivalent of withdrawing funds from a bank account without ever making a deposit. At some point, you go bankrupt.

The good news is that we can influence the way we manage our energy. By doing so skillfully, you can get more done in less time, at a higher level of quality, in a more sustainable way.

A couple of key scientific findings point the way. The first is that sleep is more important than food. You can go a week without eating and the only thing you'll lose is weight. Give up sleep for even a couple of days and you'll become completely dysfunctional. Even so, we're all too willing to trade away an hour of sleep in the false belief that it will give us one more hour of productivity. In fact, even very small amounts of sleep deprivation take a significant toll on our cognitive capacity. The notion that some of us can perform adequately with very little sleep is largely a myth. Less than 2.5 percent of the population—that's one in forty people—feels fully rested with less than seven to eight hours of sleep a night.

The second key finding is that our bodies follow what are known as ultradian rhythms—ninety-minute periods at the end of which we reach the limits of our capacity to work at the highest level. It's possible to push ourselves past ninety minutes by relying on coffee, or sugar, or by summoning our own stress hormones, but when we do so we're overriding our physiological need for intermittent rest and renewal. Eventually, there's a price to pay.

A ROUTINE THAT INCLUDES RENEWAL

What if you aligned your workday habits more closely with the natural rhythms of your body—recognizing renewal as a critical aspect of both effectiveness and sustainability in a world of rising demand?

In Zeke's case, the first thing he changed was his sleep routine. For years, he'd been going to sleep sometime after midnight. On reflection, he realized there was no good reason for staying up that late. The same was true about waking up at 5:30 a.m. He didn't have to start his day that early. It was just something he'd always done.

Instead, Zeke began winding down by 11 p.m. and turning off the lights no later than 11:30. He also began waking up an hour later, at 6:30 a.m., ensuring that he now gets at least seven hours of sleep a night. Instead of rushing out the door as he had in the past, Zeke sits down for breakfast with his wife and two daughters. On both counts, he leaves home feeling better.

Zeke also began taking a break of five or ten minutes at mid-morning—usually to chat with a colleague about something other than work. Within a week, he noticed more consistent energy levels and more capacity for focus all morning long. He also noticed he became less reactive. Following any difficult meeting, his inclination had been to fire off an e-mail to an offending party, which was almost always negative and ultimately counterproductive. With the advantage of more rest, he found he could hold his fire.

In addition, Zeke started scheduling thirty minutes in his calendar at lunchtime for a walk outside. He leaves his smartphone at his desk to avoid temptation. The walks give him a chance to recharge, but also provide precious time to reflect on the morning's meetings and anything else on his mind.

At first, Zeke worried that getting to work later and taking time to walk at lunch would make him less productive. Instead, he found himself working more efficiently when he returned, and getting more done over the course of the day.

Over time, Zeke also began making better choices about what work to take on. So long as he arrived at work already feeling tired, he instinctively put his energy into executing simple tasks. Doing so allowed him to feel productive without having to expend too much energy. It was the equivalent, he came to recognize, of a sugar high.

It was satisfying to accomplish a series of relatively simple tasks, but the pleasure didn't last for long.

Zeke now begins his days by tackling his most important task first. He focuses for sixty to ninety minutes on the challenge he believes has the greatest likelihood of adding long-term value. "These are the things that I should be doing as a leader," he says. "I just didn't get around to them before."

It's not that Zeke has it all figured out. When he travels, for example, he still sometimes abandons the rituals he's established at home. Then he has to struggle to build them back into his routine. What he now understands is that when he builds renewal into his day—when he establishes the right rhythms—everything in his life works better.

TONY SCHWARTZ *is the president and CEO of The Energy Project, a company that helps organizations fuel sustainable high performance by better meeting the needs of their employees. Tony's most recent books,* Be Excellent at Anything *and* The Power of Full Engagement *(the latter co-authored with Jim Loehr), were both New York Times bestsellers.*

→ www.theenergyproject.com

"It's not the load that breaks you down, it's the way you carry it."

MAKING ROOM
FOR SOLITUDE

—

Leo Babauta

In 1845, Henry David Thoreau set out for the woods near Walden Pond to find solitude, for his thoughts and his writing. He wanted to get away from the business and noise of nineteenth-century city life.

He wrote, "I went to the woods because I wished to live deliberately, to front only the essential facts of life, and see if I could not learn what it had to teach, and not, when I came to die, discover that I had not lived."

He went, in other words, to learn what the solitude of the woods had to teach him about living.

Today, it is essential that we find solitude so that we can learn what it has to teach us, so that we can find the quiet to listen to our inner voice, and so that we may find the space to truly focus and create.

Even a small time set aside for solitude each day—from twenty minutes to an hour—can make an enormous difference. Here we will be able to find some quiet calm when our minds are used to jumping around like a monkey in the trees. This calming of the mind helps us to figure out what really matters and to hear own creative voice, which can be drowned out by the cacophony of our daily tasks and online interactions.

CREATING THE SPACE

Set the time for your first block of solitude now—and make it an essential part of your daily routine.

For many people, the best time for solitude is early in the morning. The kids are still sleeping and everything is quiet. I get my best work done then, and the great thing is that nothing comes up that early to disrupt your schedule.

If early morning doesn't work, try doing it as soon as you arrive at the office. When I worked in an office, I'd get in a half hour to an hour early, just so I could get some quiet work done before the office started buzzing. Again, first thing is great because later, things get busy and start to disrupt your solitude block.

Many people can't create solitude at home or at the office because of constant interruptions and requests for their time. In this case it's best to get away and go to a coffee shop, library, or park where you can find quiet and—ideally—a place without wireless Internet.

A great option for the night owls among us is to use the late-night hours for solitude and distraction-free space. If you work best at night, you can find solitude by scheduling a block of time to work alone after dark.

A SIMPLE SOLITUDE PRACTICE

Most people are uncomfortable with the idea of solitude because it means facing yourself without distractions. Practice can make solitude less scary, and will help you become comfortable with the prospect of finding it on a regular basis.

One amazing way to practice is a simple meditation session once a day. Meditation doesn't have to be mystical or complicated: at heart, it's simply sitting and doing nothing else for at least a few minutes. A great place to build this into your daily routine is as soon as you wake up—get up, drink some water, and then sit and meditate for five, ten, or even twenty minutes before you start your day.

How do you meditate? Find a quiet space and sit. Stay upright, keep your eyes open but not focused on anything in particular, and breathe through your nose. Start by noticing your posture, your body. Then focus your attention on your breath, as it comes in and out of your body. Notice your thoughts coming up, acknowledge them, but don't engage with them. Always return your attention to your breath. Keep doing this for at least a few minutes, and you're done.

What's the point of sitting? There is no point—sitting *is* the point. You're not doing it to reduce stress, gain enlightenment, or learn more about yourself—though all these things might happen—but to practice just sitting. In doing so, you are practicing being alone, and doing nothing but what you're doing. This is essential.

At first meditation will be uncomfortable, but you'll get better at it. You'll learn a lot about yourself, and you'll get better at being mindful, and being comfortable in solitude.

You'll also learn to watch your thoughts and not be controlled by them. As you do, you'll have learned a key skill for focus: how to notice the urge to switch tasks and not act on that urge, but just return your attention to the task at hand. This is what you learn in solitude, and it is everything.

LEO BABAUTA *is a simplicity blogger and author. He created Zen Habits, a top blog; mnmlist.com; and the bestselling books* Focus, The Power of Less, *and* The Effortless Life.

→ www.zenhabits.net

KEY
TAKEAWAYS

—

Building a Rock-Solid Routine

Get more insights and the desktop wallpaper at:

→ www.99u.com/routines

• GREAT WORK BEFORE EVERYTHING ELSE

Do your most meaningful creative work at the beginning of your day, and leave "reactive work"—like responding to e-mail or other messages—for later.

• JUMP-START YOUR CREATIVITY

Establish "associative triggers"—such as listening to the same music or arranging your desk in a certain way—that tell your mind it's time to get down to work.

• FEEL THE FREQUENCY

Commit to working on your project at consistent intervals—ideally every day—to build creative muscle and momentum over time.

• PULSE AND PAUSE

Move rhythmically between spending and renewing your energy by working in ninety-minute bursts and then taking a break.

• GET LONELY

Make a point of spending some time alone each day. It's a way to observe unproductive habits and thought processes, and to calm your mind.

• DON'T WAIT FOR MOODS

Show up, whether you feel inspired or not.

CHAPTER TWO

FINDING FOCUS IN A DISTRACTED WORLD

–

How to hone your attention to produce work that really matters

In 1971, renowned social scientist Herbert Simon observed, "What information consumes is rather obvious: it consumes the attention of its recipients. Hence a wealth of information creates a poverty of attention."

In the decades since Simon's visionary statement, the amount of information that we're confronted with on a daily basis has grown exponentially. Open-plan offices have brought the buzz of other people's activities into our workspaces. The Internet has provided an infinite source of distraction right inside our primary workstation—the computer. And smartphones have made the allure of new information available anytime, anywhere.

Amid this constant surge of information, attention has become our most precious asset. To spend it wisely, we must develop a better understanding of how temptation works on our brains, cultivate new strategies for enhancing our self-control, and carve out time to truly focus on big, creative tasks.

In a world filled with distraction, attention is our competitive advantage. Look at each day as a challenge—and an opportunity—to keep your eye on the prize.

SCHEDULING IN TIME
FOR CREATIVE THINKING

—

Cal Newport

Since yesterday, I've received eighty-six e-mail messages, many of which require a time-consuming response. Only four of these messages directly concern the primary responsibility of my job as a university professor: publishing big new ideas.

This disparity is astonishing. And I'm not alone in my experience. Increasingly, creative minds are torn in two opposing directions. We're asked to apply our intellectual capital to solve hard problems—a creative goal that requires uninterrupted focus. At the same time, we're asked to be constantly available by e-mail and messenger and in meetings—an administrative goal that creates constant distraction. We're being asked, in other words, to simultaneously resist and embrace distraction to advance in our careers—a troubling paradox.

I believe that this phenomenon has a lot to do with the lack of clear metrics in the knowledge work sector. Consider the example of a computer programmer being bombarded with "urgent" e-mail messages from a manager. The obligation of the programmer to constantly monitor his inbox undoubtedly reduces the amount and quality of code he produces, which in turn reduces the value being generated by the company. But this value is ambiguous and is hard to measure precisely. The manager, therefore, is unlikely to be reprimanded for his distracting e-mails, as there is no clear evidence of their damage.

In a business environment, people will resort to whatever makes their life easier—like firing off e-mails to subordinates at the drop of a hat—until someone higher up demands that a particular behavior stops. It's hard, however, for someone higher up to make such a demand without clear evidence of exactly how much the behavior is costing the organization. Because of this lack of clear metrics, we've sunk into a productivity morass, where the focus in adopting a new administrative practice is on short-term convenience rather than long-term value.

In 2009, the literary critic John Freeman wrote a provocative book, *The Tyranny of E-mail*, proposing that this communication technology has caused more harm than good. The review of Freeman's book in the *New York Times* captures the standard dismissal of such critiques:

"By John Freeman's lights, [the fact that I send group e-mails] makes me a bad guy," the reviewer wrote. He then points to a specific e-mail, and replies: "And the problem is? In this case I asked a question and got helpful responses."[2]

In other words, the reviewer rejects Freeman's argument that group e-mails consume a disproportionate amount of our time by countering that he had recently sent such an e-mail and had received useful replies in return. This is the essence of our convenience addiction: because we lack clear metrics for these behaviors' costs, we cannot weigh their pros against their cons. Therefore, the evidence of any benefit is enough to justify continued use. Though group e-mails might be costing a company thousands of man-hours of value-producing deep thought, this mind-set argues, if such e-mails occasionally make an employee's life easier, they should be allowed to continue.

$$\sim\!\!\infty\!\!\sim$$

Now that we better understand how we ended up in our current productivity paradox, we're left to consider solutions. In the long run, we can hope to reform our administrative practices, keeping only what maximizes our ability to do meaningful work. But we shouldn't expect such a major transformation to happen anytime soon. We are left then to consider individual habits that will preserve our ability to apply undistracted focus to valuable problems while still making us available enough that we do not annoy our coworkers.

This is a problem I've studied and written about for years. I've seen many different proposals for how to preserve focused work in a hectic schedule. Of these many proposed tactics, one stands out, in my experience, as being unusually effective. I call this the focus block method, and it works, ironically, by turning the machinery of the distraction culture against itself.

THE POWER OF DAILY FOCUS BLOCKS

The focus block method leverages the well-understood concept of a pre-scheduled appointment. It has you block off a substantial chunk of time, most days of the week, for applying sustained focus to your most important creative tasks. This scheduling usually happens at the beginning of a new week or at the end of the previous week. The key twist is that you mark this time on your calendar like any other meeting. This is especially important if your organization uses a shared calendar system.

Now, when someone tries to schedule something during these times, you can defer to your existing, clearly marked obligation: "Sorry, I'm already booked from nine to twelve that day." Similarly, if someone complains that you were slow to respond to an e-mail, or didn't pick up the phone, you have a socially acceptable excuse: "I was booked all morning and am just seeing this now." People are used to the idea that they cannot demand your attention during times when you already have a scheduled appointment. The focus block technique takes advantage of this understanding to buy you some time for undistracted focus without the need for excessive apology or explanation.

Blocking off time for uninterrupted focus, however, is only half the battle. The other half is resisting distraction. This means: no e-mail, no Internet, and no phone. This sounds easy in theory, but can be surprisingly hard to embrace in practice. If you've been immersed in distraction for years, you need to train yourself before you can work for long periods without it. A few tips can help you in this effort:

Start with small blocks of focused time and then gradually work yourself up to longer durations. A good rule of thumb is to begin with an hour at a time, then add fifteen minutes to each session every two weeks. The key, however, is to *never* allow distraction. If you give in and quickly check Facebook, cancel the whole block and try again later. Your mind can never come to believe that even a little bit of distraction is okay during these blocks.

Tackle a clearly identified and isolated task. If you have to write an article, for example, do the research ahead of time, so that when you get to your focus block you can put your word processor in full-screen mode and turn your entire attention to your prose.

Consider using a different location for these blocks. Move to a different room, or a library, or even a quiet place outside to perform your focused work. When possible, do your work with pen and paper to avoid even the possibility of online distraction.

The battle between focus and distraction is a serious problem—both to the competitiveness of our companies and to our own sanity. The amount of value lost to unchecked use of convenient but distracting work habits is staggering. The focus block method described above does not fix this problem, but it does give you a way to push back against its worst excesses, systematically producing important creative work even when your environment seems designed to thwart this goal.

CAL NEWPORT *is a writer and a professor at Georgetown University. His most recent book,* So Good They Can't Ignore You, *argues that "follow your passion" is bad advice. Find out more about Cal and his writing at his blog, Study Hacks.*

→ calnewport.com/blog

"It is not enough to be busy, (THE ANTS ARE BUSY) we must ask: 'What are we busy about?'"

BANISHING MULTITASKING FROM OUR REPERTOIRE

—

Christian Jarrett

Author Jonathan Franzen takes the temptation of multitasking so seriously that, to write his best-selling novel *Freedom*, he locked himself away in a sparsely furnished office. As he told *Time* magazine, he went so far as to strip his vintage laptop of its wireless card and surgically destroy its Ethernet port with superglue and a saw. He then established a cocoon-like environment with earplugs and noise-cancelling headphones.

A little extreme, perhaps, but Franzen demonstrated shrewd insight into human fallibility. Creative minds are highly susceptible to distraction, and our newfound connectivity poses a powerful temptation for all of us to drift off focus.

THE MULTITASKING MYTH

Studies show that the human mind can only truly multitask when it comes to highly automatic behaviors like walking. For activities that require conscious attention, there is really no such thing as multitasking, only *task switching*—the process of flicking the mind back and forth between different demands. It can feel as though we're super-efficiently doing two or more things at once. But in fact we're just doing one thing, then another, then back again, with significantly less skill and accuracy than if we had simply focused on one job at a time.

Take the example of reading. Where once we might have spent a few hours with a book and then sought out social contact, tools like Instant Messenger offer the tantalizing possibility of doing both at once. The reality? Laura Bowman and her team at Central Connecticut State University found that students using IM while reading a textbook took about 25 percent longer to read the passage (not including the time spent on IM), compared with students who simply read.[3] Whatever the specific arrangement, whether it's reading plus IM or writing plus TV, the end result is the same—performance quality suffers and all activities take longer to do than they would have if a single task had been the sole focus.

BACKGROUND DISTRACTIONS

Of course, double-tasking isn't our only affliction. Perhaps even more insidious is our habit of superficially committing to focused work while leaving e-mail or social media sites open in the background. All it takes is a whistle from one of these apps offering the thrill of an unexpected communication, and bam, we're off course.

But we don't just lose the time spent answering a message when this happens; we also struggle to rediscover the "flow" we were enjoying before we were disturbed. A dramatic demonstration of this appeared in an experiment in the offices of Microsoft, where the working patterns of twenty-seven employees were monitored over a two-week period. Not only did replying to messages divert workers for an average of ten minutes, they also tended to use the break as a chance to cycle through a range of other applications, meaning another ten or fifteen minutes went by on average before they finally resumed their primary task. Sometimes the diversion lasted hours.[4]

We may tell ourselves that we'll just answer one quick e-mail or make one short phone call. But in reality, switching tasks sends us down a rabbit hole, pulling our attention away from our priority work for much longer than we anticipate.

Even if you have cast-iron willpower, the mere fact that the Internet is lying in wait on your computer takes a toll on your work performance. The very act of resisting temptations eats up concentration and leaves you mentally depleted. Psychologists demonstrated this in a 2011 study. Participants at the University of Copenhagen were told to perform a computer task. Afterward, some of them were allowed to watch a funny video, while the others were faced with a play button for the video, but had to resist pressing it (akin to a tempting YouTube clip on your computer). When confronted with an additional task afterward, those who had to resist the video performed worse than those who were allowed to watch it.[5]

In short, committing to ignore distractions is rarely enough. Like Franzen, we must strive to remove them entirely from our field of attention. Otherwise, we'll end up using half our mental energy just keeping ourselves from breaking our own rules.

THE HANGOVER EFFECT

No matter how much we think we're in control, our brains have their own agenda. Let's say you're working on a writing project in the morning and—for the sake of variety—you decide to leave it unfinished and work on a creative brief in the afternoon. This may seem like a harmless change of pace, but research has shown that the unfinished morning task could linger in your mind like a mental itch, adversely affecting your performance later on—an effect that psychologists call "attentional residue".

One study that demonstrated this involved participants completing two different assignments: a word puzzle first, and then a completely separate recruitment task that involved looking at résumés. Once participants had begun reviewing the résumés—that is, once they had mentally switched onto the new task—researcher Sophie Leroy surprised them with a challenge that involved judging whether strings of letters were real words or not.

Participants who hadn't been allowed to finish the puzzle task responded more quickly to words that had been featured in it, or that reflected its goals (e.g., "solve"). Because they hadn't finished that first task, it was still niggling away in their minds. Not surprisingly, Leroy found this hangover effect had a detrimental effect on participants' performance on the résumé task compared with participants who had been allowed to finish the initial word puzzle.[6]

While it feels easy enough to put one task on hold to start

another, studies like this are a reminder that we find it very difficult to let go of unfinished challenges. They continue to draw on our mental resources even after we think we've switched focus. What's more, attempting to ignore this mental tug drains us even further.

If you can, it's best to find a good stopping point on a project—one that frees your mind from nagging questions—before moving on to another task. That way, you'll find it easier to achieve mental closure and apply all your energy to the next challenge.

Of course, there are times in the creative process when it does pay to switch things up. When you're at the problem-solving stage or you need to generate new ideas, psychologists have shown that taking your mind off-task briefly can help your subconscious find links between disparate concepts.

But this is an exception to the general rule that multitasking is a productivity drag masquerading as an efficiency booster. Once you've cooked up your ideas and identified the way forward, it's time for the real labor of love. For that, you need single-minded focus.

DR. CHRISTIAN JARRETT *is a psychologist and author of* The Rough Guide to Psychology. *He writes the Research* Digest *blog for the British Psychological Society and is staff writer on its house magazine,* The Psychologist.

→ www.psychologywriter.org.uk

"The most basic form of human stupidity is forgetting what we are trying to accomplish."

— FRIEDRICH NIETZSCHE

Q&A:

UNDERSTANDING OUR COMPULSIONS

—

with Dan Ariely

Dan Ariely is fascinated by the irrational. A leading behavioral economist, professor, and bestselling author, Ariely researches topics such as why we make poor decisions, why we cheat, and why we lie—even when it's not necessarily in our best interest. He is also the founder and director of the cheekily named Center for Advanced Hindsight. We talked to him about the science behind the irrational urges that drive us to fritter away our most valuable time at work—and how we can fight back.

In your research, you explore why we make bad decisions—often unintentionally. Can you talk about how this impacts us in the workplace?

First, people have a really bad habit of coming in and checking e-mail first thing in the morning. And for many people, the morning is the most productive time. E-mail is very, very tempting, so they basically sacrifice their productive time for e-mail.

The second issue is that in doing things, we like to feel that we're making progress. So if you get to erase ten e-mails from your inbox, you feel like you have achieved something. But if you think carefully about it, it's not clear that you're going to get something out of it.

The next thing working against us is the calendar. It has a tendency to represent tasks that can fit in thirty-minute or one-hour blocks. And tasks that take, say, fifty hours—which could be how long it takes you to complete a meaningful creative task—don't naturally get represented in that calendar.

Then there's opportunity cost. With money, opportunity cost is the fact that every time you spend three dollars on a latte, you're not going to spend it on something else. With time, there is also an opportunity cost—but it's often even harder to understand.

Every time you're doing something, you're not doing something else. But you don't really see what it is that you're giving up. Especially when it comes to, let's say, e-mail versus doing something that takes fifty hours. It is very easy for you to see the e-mail. It is not that easy for you to see the thing that takes fifty hours.

Why is e-mail such a great temptation system?

The psychologist B. F. Skinner came up with the idea of random reinforcement, where you give a rat a lever and every hundred times it presses the lever, it gets a piece of food. For the rat, that is exciting. But if the number is a random number—any number between one and one hundred—it actually ends up being more exciting. And the rat keeps on working much, much more, even if you take the reward away altogether.

I think that e-mail and social networks are a great example of random reinforcement. Usually, when we pull the lever to check our e-mail, it's not that interesting. But, from time to time, it's exciting. And that excitement, which happens at random intervals, keeps us coming back to check our e-mail all the time.

Another thing to understand is the notion of choice architecture, which means that the environment in which we make decisions tends to have a lot to do with what our final decisions are. So if you're in line at the buffet, the way the food is organized—whether the fresh fruit and salad is easily accessible or tucked in the back behind more tempting options—will determine what you end up eating.

If you think about it, the world around us, including the world in our computers, is all about trying to tempt us to do things *right now*. Take Facebook, for example. Do they want you to be more productive twenty years from now? Or do they want to take your time, attention, and money right now? The same thing goes for YouTube, online newspapers, and so on.

The basic combination of these three things: (1) that the world around us tries to tempt us; (2) that we listen to the world around us (e.g., choice architecture); and (3) that we don't deal very well with temptation . . . if you put all of those things together, you have a recipe for disaster.

So what do we do?

I think the general notion is that, when temptation hits, it's going to be incredibly hard for us to resist. So if your e-mail is running and it is telling you that a message is waiting for you, that's going to be very hard to resist. In your mind, you'll keep thinking about what exciting things are waiting for you. Now, if you never opened your e-mail, you would do much better.

It would probably be best if managers went to the IT department and asked that e-mail not be distributed between eight and eleven every morning. The idea that the best way to communicate with people is 24/7 is not really an idea about maximizing productivity.

Do you think our ability to exercise self-control— to resist temptation—is limited?

Self-control has two elements. There are self-control problems and self-control solutions. Self-control problems are all about "now versus later."

There was a study by Ralph Keeney showing that if you estimate what percentage of human mortality comes from bad decision-making it will be about 10 percent for people a hundred years ago. If you look at it these days, it is a little bit more than 40 percent. Why? Because as we invent new technologies, we also invent new ways to kill ourselves. Think about obesity. Think about smoking. Think about texting and driving. All of those are self-control problems.

Self-control solutions are all the things we try in order to get ourselves to behave better. We think that if we pay a lot of money to join the gym, we will feel guilty and we will keep going. It turns out that guilt does work—but only short-term. Eventually, the guilt goes away. We buy hundred-calorie cookie packs. Because we think that if it's just a small pack, we will eat fewer cookies, and so on.

Then finally, there is ego depletion, which deals with what happens throughout the day as we resist temptation over and over. The results show that it takes energy to resist each temptation, and that as we use more and more of this energy as the day goes on, we have less and less of it left, which increases the chances that we will give in to temptation.

What should we focus on to help us manage our time better?

I think one of the biggest factors is progression markers. For many things, it's hard to figure out how much progress you're making. When you answer a thousand e-mails, you see every e-mail you answer. When you are thinking about a difficult problem, it feels like maybe there were thirty wasted hours and then finally you had a half hour at the end that was useful—because the idea kind of came to you.

There isn't a linear progression and a sense of progress. So I think the big question is: how do we make ourselves feel like we're making progress? Because if you can create that progress, I think many of the other things would become smaller barriers.

If you're working with a pen, you have evidence of all the things you've done. You can see your path. But if you work on a computer, it's just the current state of the work—you don't have the previous versions.

If that's the case, you could think about some tricks to remind yourself about your progress. Maybe we should keep a diary? Maybe we should keep older versions of our efforts? Maybe every day we make a new version of a document we are working on so that we can keep a visible record of our progress?

DAN ARIELY, *James B. Duke Professor of Psychology and Behavioral Economics at Duke University, is dedicated to helping people live more sensible—if not more rational—lives. He is a founding member of the Center for Advanced Hindsight and author of the New York Times bestsellers* Predictably Irrational, The Upside of Irrationality, *and* The Honest Truth About Dishonesty.

→ www.danariely.com

"Creation is in part merely the business of forgoing the great and small distractions."

— E.B. WHITE

LEARNING TO CREATE AMIDST CHAOS

—

Erin Rooney Doland

Leigh Michaels, prolific author of more than eighty romance novels, once said that "waiting for inspiration to write is like standing at the airport waiting for a train." Conditions to produce one's craft are rarely ideal, and waiting for everything to be perfect is almost always an exercise in procrastination.

Most celebrated creative minds don't have wealthy patrons who support their lives and proclivities regardless of what they produce. Musicians have day jobs, poets are also professors, and feature filmmakers shoot commercials on the side. Like it or not, we are constantly forced to juggle tasks and battle unwanted distractions—to truly set ourselves apart, we must learn to be creative amidst chaos.

POSITIVE DISTRACTION

Negative distractions that interfere with creative work can come in many forms: the television set, undone chores, social media, e-mail, coworkers who want to gossip, anxieties, self-doubt. Removing oneself from all of this interference is theoretically possible—the Yaddo colony has certainly served as a temporary, interruption-free retreat for hundreds of the great artists—but is unfeasible for most of us. Beyond this, abandoning one's responsibilities at home and the office while taking up residence at an artists' retreat is impractical and potentially irresponsible. Plus, there is that pesky truth that anxieties and self-doubt can multiply when fed with silence and an abundance of time.

Researchers at Stanford University discovered in the 1970s that one of the best ways to combat negative distractions is simply to embrace positive distractions. In short, we can fight bad distractions with good distractions.

In the Stanford study,[7] children were given an option to eat one marshmallow right away, or wait a few minutes and receive two marshmallows. The children who were able to delay their gratification employed positive distraction techniques to be successful. Some children sang; others kicked the table; they simply did whatever they needed to do to get their minds focused on something other than the marshmallows.

There are many ways to use positive distraction techniques for more than just resisting marshmallows. Set a timer and race the clock to complete a task. Tie unrelated rewards to accomplishments—get a drink from the break room or log on to social media for three minutes after reaching a milestone. Write down every invading and negatively distracting thought and schedule a ten-minute review session later in the day to focus on these anxieties and lay them to rest.

SELF-CONTROL

Still, it takes a significant amount of self-control to work in a chaotic environment. Ignoring negative distractions to focus on preferred activities requires energy and mental agility. For his book *Willpower*, psychologist Roy Baumeister analyzed findings from hundreds of experiments to determine why some people can retain focus for hours, while others can't. He discovered that self-control is not genetic or fixed, but rather a skill one can develop and improve with practice.[8]

Baumeister suggests many strategies for increasing self-control. One of these strategies is to develop a seemingly unrelated habit, such as improving your posture or saying "yes" instead of "yeah" or flossing your teeth every night before bed. This can strengthen your willpower in other areas of your life. Additionally, once the new habit is ingrained and can be completed without much effort or thought, that energy can then be turned to other activities requiring more self-control. Tasks done on autopilot don't use up our stockpile of energy like tasks that have to be consciously completed.

Entertaining activities, such as playing strategic games that require concentration and have rules that change as the game advances, or listening to audio books that require attention to follow along with the plot, can also be used to increase attention. Even simple behaviors like regularly getting a good night's sleep are shown to improve focus and self-control.

MINDFUL VS. MINDLESS WORK

As much as we cultivate it, however, self-control is still finite—so we must combine this approach with other strategies. Two researchers at the University of California, Davis, Drs. Kimberly Elsbach and Andrew Hargadon, discovered that creativity and efficiency can be enhanced over the course of a workday when workers alternate between mindful and mindless activities. To relate it to physical exercise, the human mind is better suited for running sprints than marathons.

Their report in the journal *Organization Science* identified activities such as "simple manufacturing line tasks (e.g., filling supply bins), making photocopies, simple cleaning chores (e.g., cleaning laboratory equipment), performing simple maintenance tasks, sorting or collating tasks, and simple service tasks (e.g., unpacking and stocking supplies)" as "mindless" work. Conversely, the core tasks of problem-solving and invention that relate to one's job or creative pursuits are "mindful." Shifting from mindful to mindless work gives the brain time to process complex problems in a relaxed state and also restores the energy necessary for the next round of mindful work.[9]

Every person has a different length of time he or she can work before productivity and efficiency begin to decline—and this length of time can also shift over the course of a day. Keeping track of when energy levels rise and fall will help determine a schedule for alternating between mindful and mindless activities. Once these ebbs and flows are determined, a timer can be used to keep track of, and direct, these shifts to help prevent exhaustion and time-wasting.

Given all this talk of tracking and training, it might sound like you need to be a scientist or an athlete to truly excel at making great creative work. And in a sense you do: any kind of excellence ultimately requires observation, refinement, adaptation, and endurance. Just listen to acclaimed writer Haruki Murakami explaining the self-control he must put forth to complete his work:

> When I'm in writing mode for a novel, I get up at four a.m. and work for five to six hours. In the afternoon, I run for ten kilometers or swim for fifteen-hundred meters (or do both), then I read a bit and listen to some music. I go to bed at nine p.m. I keep to this routine every day without variation. The repetition itself becomes the important thing; it's a form of mesmerism. I mesmerize myself to reach a deeper state of mind. But to hold to such repetition for so long—six months to a year—requires a good amount of mental and physical strength. In that sense, writing a long novel is like survival training. Physical strength is as necessary as artistic sensitivity.[10]

Just as a basketball player making a free throw on a rival team's court has to train his body to perform despite the screaming crowd, creative minds must learn to train their attention and marshal their creative energies under the most chaotic circumstances.

ERIN ROONEY DOLAND *is editor-in-chief of Unclutterer.com, a website providing daily articles on home and office organization, and author of the book* Unclutter Your Life in One Week. *She is a writer, productivity consultant, and lecturer. Writing and simple living are two of her greatest passions.*

→ www.unclutterer.com

"Tell me to what you pay attention and I will tell you who you are."

— JOSÉ ORTEGA Y GASSET

TUNING IN TO YOU

—

Scott Belsky

What's the first thing you do when you get out of a meeting or a class? When you're walking between conference rooms? When you're waiting in line? These in-between moments used to be opportunities to pause and reflect. Now, we eagerly jump into the communication stream, tuning in to the world instead of tuning in to ourselves.

We rarely—if ever—think about the cost of doing this. So what if you take a few minutes to check your text messages? You can pass the time by flipping through your phone, or by taking a moment to look around and think, right? What difference does it make?

Diving into my device engages me. Whether I'm communicating with others or checking website stats, it's an intentional activity that will have a specific, often gratifying, outcome. By contrast, doing nothing during these moments of downtime feels less intentional. It's an unfocused activity with no clear outcome—I am just being present in the moment, with my eyes and mind wide open.

I would argue that taking time to experience the flip side of connected, intentional activity—to disengage from the stream and truly be present in the now—is crucial to the well-being and performance of creative minds. Consider it "filling the well," as poet and artist Julia Cameron once put it. When we turn off one type of stimuli, we unleash another.

RENEW YOUR INTEREST IN YOURSELF

Many years ago, while still in school, I spent a semester in Vermont at a program called the Mountain School. As part of the experience there, every student completes a three-day solo journey in the wilderness. They provide you with a tarp and other necessities and then send you off to hike to a camping spot in the Green Mountains. Just a few rules: no music, no electronics, and no company.

It should come as no surprise that my first day alone was extremely boring. I had no one to talk to, nothing to read or watch. I just sat there, mind blank. The constant external stimulation I had been depending on my entire life had suddenly ceased. My mind didn't know what to do with itself.

On the second day, however, something changed. My brain suddenly reactivated. I became truly aware of my surroundings: The quiet of an early April snowfall. The grandeur of century-old trees. The hours flew past.

What I learned during my solo experience was that my thinking—my creativity and imagination—reached a new velocity as soon as I unplugged. When you tune in to the moment, you begin to recognize the world around you and the true potential of your own mind.

PRESERVE UNSTRUCTURED TIME

There's no executive in the digital era better known for long-term planning than Jeff Bezos, founder and CEO of Amazon. In the early days of the company, when future-thinking was perhaps most important, Bezos would try to keep his schedule completely open on Mondays and Thursdays. Rather than playing catch-up or taking on a typical CEO schedule of back-to-back meetings, Bezos preserved a good chunk of his weekly time just to explore, learn, and think. He would poke around the various Amazon sites and spend time on the stuff he would ordinarily never get to do.

As Bezos explained in a *WIRED* profile, "I wander around and talk to people or set up my own meetings—ones that are not part of the regular calendar."[11] Setting aside this unstructured time to fully invest in inhabiting the present moment—to take the tenor of his team or fully dive into his own thoughts—has no doubt served Bezos well in honing Amazon's long-term vision.

Most of us find very little time to casually explore, follow our whims, or think big, but this capacity is a major competitive advantage in the era of constant connectivity. Maybe we can't carve out whole days for ourselves like Bezos did, but preserving pockets of time to unplug—perhaps a couple of hours in the morning a few days a week—can be transformative.

OPEN YOURSELF TO SERENDIPITY

Chance encounters can also provide enormous benefits for your projects—and your life. Being friendly while standing in line for coffee at a conference might lead to a conversation, a business card exchange, and the first investment in your company a few months later. The person sitting next to you at a concert who chats you up during intermission might end up becoming your largest customer. Or, two strangers sitting in a nail salon exchanging stories about their families might lead to a blind date, which might lead to a marriage. (This is how I met my wife. Lucky for me, neither stranger had a smartphone, so they resorted to matchmaking.)

I am consistently humbled and amazed by just how much creation and realization is the product of serendipity. Of course, these chance opportunities must be noticed and pursued for them to have any value. It makes you wonder how much we regularly miss. As we tune in to our devices during every moment of transition, we are letting the incredible potential of serendipity pass us by.

The greatest value of any experience is often found in its seams. The primary benefits of a conference often have nothing to do with what happens onstage. The true reward of a trip to the nail salon may be more than the manicure.

When you value the power of serendipity, you start noticing it at work right away. Try leaving the smartphone in your pocket the next time you're in line or in a crowd. Notice one source of unexpected value on every such occasion. Develop the discipline to allow for serendipity.

PRIORITIZE BEING PRESENT

Today's challenge is to keep your focus and preserve the sanctity of mind required to create, and to ultimately make an impact in what matters most to you. This can only happen when you capitalize on the here and now. To do this, alternate periods of connectedness with periods of truly being present:

Be aware of the cost of constant connection. If your focus is always on others—and quenching your appetite for information and external validation—you will miss out on the opportunity to mine the potential of your own mind.

Recognize when you're tuning in to the stream for the wrong reasons. We often look to our devices for a sense of reassurance. Become more aware of the insecurity that pulls you away from the present. You cannot imagine what will be if you are constantly concerned with what already is.

Create windows of non-stimulation in your day. Make this time sacred and use it to focus on a separate list of two or three things that are important to you over the long term. Use this time to think, to digest what you've learned, and to plan.

Listen to your gut as much as you listen to others. With all the new sources of communication and amplification, don't let yourself be persuaded by the volume of the masses. Nothing should resonate more loudly than your own intuition.

Stay open to the possibilities of serendipity. The most important connections—whether with people, ideas, or mistakes that lead to key realizations—often spring from unexpected circumstances. By being fully present where you are, you let chance (and the curious universe we live in) work its magic.

You are the steward of your own potential. The resources within you—and around you—are only tapped when you recognize their value and develop ways to use them. Whatever the future of technology may hold, the greatest leaders will be those most capable of tuning in to themselves and harnessing the full power of their own minds.

SCOTT BELSKY is Adobe's Vice President of Community and Co-Founder & Head of Behance, the leading online platform for creatives to showcase and discover creative work. Scott has been called one of the "100 Most Creative People in Business" by Fast Company, and is the author of the international bestselling book, Making Ideas Happen. *He is also an investor and advisor for several companies including Pinterest and Uber.*

→ www.scottbelsky.com

KEY
TAKEAWAYS

—

Finding Focus in a Distracted World

Get more insights and the desktop wallpaper at:

→ www.99u.com/focus

- ## DEFEND YOUR CREATIVE TIME
  Book time on your calendar for uninterrupted, focused work—and respect those blocks of time as you would any client meeting.

- ## FOCUS WHEN YOU'RE FRESH
  Tackle the projects that require "hard focus" early in your day. Self-control—and our ability to resist distractions—declines as the day goes on.

- ## KILL THE BACKGROUND NOISE
  Turn off your phone, e-mail, and any apps unrelated to your task. Even the presence of background activity (and temptation) can drain your focus.

- ## MAKE PROGRESS VISIBLE
  Marking progress is a huge motivator for long-term projects. Make your daily achievements visible by saving iterations, posting milestones, or keeping a daily journal.

- ## GIVE YOUR BRAIN A BREAK
  Alternate challenging creative work with more "mindless" tasks to give your brain time to rest and refuel.

- ## TAP INTO TRANSITIONAL MOMENTS
  Take a break from checking your smartphone during transitional moments, and open yourself up to opportunity and serendipity.

CHAPTER THREE

TAMING
YOUR
TOOLS

–

*How to gracefully manage
new technologies for better
workflow and well-being*

Technology should be a tool, but if we do not keep our wits about us, it can easily become our taskmaster. As WIRED magazine co-founder Kevin Kelly has written, "Every new technology will bite back. The more powerful its gifts, the more powerfully it can be abused."

Our current relationship with technology is fraught. We feel overwhelmed and out of control. We dream of declaring "e-mail bankruptcy" or maybe "going off the grid." But we are also addicted and entranced—constantly logging on to share our every thought, image, and idea.

It's easy to blame the tools, but the real problem is us. Rather than demonizing new technologies unnecessarily or championing them blindly, we must begin to develop a subtler sensibility.

We must ask hard questions like: Why are we driven to use our tools so compulsively? What would it mean to approach e-mail and social media mindfully? How does being tethered to our devices impact our physical bodies—and even our imaginations?

In this new era of technological invention, questioning how we work—which behaviors are productive and which are destructive—is an essential part of the creative process.

MAKING E-MAIL MATTER

—

Aaron Dignan

Inbox zero. It sounds pretty good, doesn't it? And why not—we send and receive more e-mail today than ever before, and that volume continues to increase with each passing year. A recent study by the McKinsey Global Institute found that the average knowledge worker spends 28 percent of his or her workweek either writing, reading, or responding to e-mail.[12] No matter what kind of work you do, chances are you spend far too much energy dealing with your inbox.

As a result, many of us are on a permanent mission to reduce our e-mail workload, and this has translated into a bit of an e-mail efficiency craze. That desire has been fueled by literally hundreds of tools, techniques, services, plug-ins, and extensions to help you manage your e-mail. As a result, e-mail "best practices" are getting pretty exhausting to follow. According to productivity thought leaders, to master your e-mail, you need to do most (if not all) of the following:

- Label your e-mails for faster retrieval

- Set up rules so that your e-mail can sort itself

- Archive all of your e-mails so that you can focus

- Color code your e-mail, for visual cues to priority

- Use a reminder tool so that important e-mail chains resurface

- Convert e-mail into tasks, so that nothing slips through the cracks

- Track e-mail, so you can see when/where it gets read

- Create e-mail templates so that you can rapidly send common messages

- Unsubscribe from excess newsletters frequently

- Limit your e-mails to five sentences or less

- Use a social plug-in so that you can see the faces and facts behind your e-mails

How has it come to this? Why is e-mail such a complex communication channel? The reason is that e-mail has become our primary input/

output mechanism for conversation, ideas, reminders, information, events, video, images, and documents. In our physical absence, it is a digital representation of us, a permanent location for the rest of the working world to drop their needs at our feet.

Because of this, our e-mail represents a sort of digital extension of our brain. Sure, social media and mobile have drawn some of this attention and volume (and for the next generation perhaps they'll grab it all), but that doesn't change the fact that each of us will always maintain a digital inbox somewhere, and that's going to be where the action is. The bottleneck occurs because our digital selves—you@gmail.com—can handle far more input than our physical selves. And short of dramatic increases in artificial intelligence, we're going to need to solve for the difference ourselves.

When I think about my inbox as an extension of my brain, the notion of inbox zero becomes both more meaningful and more elusive. A rush to a clean inbox might leave me empty, if the e-mails themselves don't trigger the development and progression of my ideas and goals. Put more simply, I don't want to simply beat back my e-mail every day like some pointless enemy. I want to ensure that the time spent with my e-mail adds up to something—that it helps me achieve more. After all, why am I reading and writing all this e-mail in the first place?!

With each e-mail that arrives, there is a moment when you must decide how to contextualize the message: Is this something I need to know? Something that requires an urgent response? Something I need to come back to later? Something that a friend might enjoy? Something that requires action? Something that requires thought and reflection? And what other e-mails, ideas, tasks, and projects already in play might it relate to? To make the most of your inbox, I recommend three simple steps:

KNOW YOUR COMPLEX GOALS

Many of us have a running list of things we'd like to accomplish, and the vast majority of these things are simple tasks. *Organize desk. E-mail Fred about the deadline. Send invoice.* Above that, we have an ever-evolving list of objectives, plans, and aspirations that are harder to wrap our heads around because they require a host of complex actions and involve multiple milestones over time.

These complex goals are elusive, subject to the ebb and flow of our time, energy, and opportunities. Some of us want to write a book. Others want to visit Peru. Still others want to meet a personal idol. Future businesses, charities, and even relationships get lost in this amorphous place simply because these things are difficult to attack in discrete tasks day after day. In order to make your inbox a catalyst to achieve these goals, you've got to put them in your line of sight. Every four months or so, I identify my two or three complex goals and tape a list of them to my desk as a constant reminder.

CONNECT THE DOTS

Any e-mail you receive might be a stepping-stone to your goal, depending on the subject and the sender. By knowing your complex goals and keeping them front and center in your mind, you can start to see relationships and potential in the content, people, and opportunities hitting your inbox.

Don't mindlessly blast through your inbox—give each message that extra moment of careful consideration to see how it might relate to your overall goals. Who could you share this with? What could you say that would move the ball forward? Is this an opportunity to ask for help or advice? Is this person a possible champion for you? With that in mind, you can label, file, forward, respond, and archive with a new kind of purpose—an eye on the long-term while you keep your head above water.

LET THINGS GO

If you're like me, you have far too many things you want to do, read, see, test, and experience. Your inbox is a treasure trove of possibilities. To a creative mind, that's very enticing. It's easy for an optimist to keep fifty, a hundred, or even a thousand e-mails hovering in their inbox in the hopes that, someday soon, they'll get a chance to give each opportunity the precious time that it deserves. But guess what? That's never gonna happen.

The most important rule in achieving your goals via your inbox is that distracting opportunities have to die for your most important goals to live. As you move through your inbox, if an idea or opportunity is catching your eye and asking for your focus, think hard about whether pursuing it will help you achieve your complex goals. If not, or if you're not sure, decline graciously and live to fight another day. If it's truly the game-changing opportunity that your optimistic inner voice says it is, chances are it will come your way again one day.

AARON DIGNAN is the CEO of the digital strategy firm Undercurrent, where he advises global brands and complex organizations like GE, American Express, Ford Motor Company, and the Cooper-Hewitt on their future in an increasingly technophilic world. He is also the author of Game Frame: Using Games as a Strategy for Success.

→ www.undercurrent.com

"The difference between successful people and very successful people is that very successful people say 'no' to almost everything."

USING SOCIAL MEDIA MINDFULLY

—

Lori Deschene

You can leverage it to make new contacts or expand your business. You can use it to showcase your expertise, share what you've learned, or learn from people you admire and respect. You can use it to stay informed, entertained, and connected. You can even find inspiration in 140 characters or less.

Psychologists suggest that social media appeals to such a wide range of people because it fulfills our most fundamental needs, including a sense of belonging and self-esteem. We all want to feel like we're part of something larger than ourselves, and we all want to believe that what we do matters.

Still, while social media helps us engage and expand our world as never before, it also presents a number of new challenges. As with any tool, we must be careful to use it for our benefit and not our detriment.

LOGGING ON WITH INTENTION

Purposeful action requires clear intentions. But we've all logged on to a social network without them. We may have been procrastinating and looking for a distraction, or feeling angry, annoyed, or frustrated and seeking to escape that feeling. Research shows that we actually get a small rush of endorphins—the same brain chemicals we enjoy after completing intense exercise—when we receive a new message. Talking about ourselves also triggers the reward center of our brains, making it even more compelling to narrate our daily activities.[13]

Whatever our reasons for turning to social media, we have abundant opportunity to do it now that most of us carry powerful mini-computers in our purses or pockets. We're always connected, always ready to discover, consume, and share information. If something's trending, we want to know about it. If someone shares something, we want to see it. And if we ever step away from the stream for a while, we feel even more pressure to catch up on everything once we've returned.

With one eye on our gadgets, we're unable to give our full attention to who and what is in front of us—meaning that we miss out on the details of our lives, ironically, while responding to our fear of missing out.

For many of us, mindlessness is the default state. It takes a concerted effort to be mindful with social media—to be proactive instead of reactive. When we're mindful, we're aware of *why* we're logging on, and we're able to fully disconnect when we've followed through with our intention. We're able to engage authentically and meaningfully, but we're not dependent on that connection in a way that limits our effectiveness and our sense of presence.

BECOMING AWARE

In order to change our relationship to social media, we need to understand how we're motivated to use it and why. Without self-awareness, we are at the mercy of our screens and feeds, pulled toward them for instant gratification when other choices might better meet our actual needs.

We can start developing self-awareness by setting boundaries for how and when we use our technology, and then checking in with our intentions when we feel compelled to use it differently. This could mean signing on only at certain predetermined times and asking ourselves key questions if we feel drawn toward our gadgets in between those times. Those questions might include:

- Is it necessary to share this? Will it add value to my life and for other people?

- Can I share this experience later so I can focus on living it now?

- Am I looking for validation? Is there something I could do to validate myself?

- Am I avoiding something I need to do instead of addressing why I don't want to do it?

- Am I feeling bored? Is there something else I could do to feel more purposeful and engaged in my day?

- Am I feeling lonely? Have I created opportunities for meaningful connection in my day?

- Am I afraid of missing out? Is the gratification of giving in to that fear worth missing out on what's in front of me?

- Am I overwhelming myself, trying to catch up? Can I let go of yesterday's conversation and join today's instead?

- Can I use this time to simply be instead of looking for something to do to fill it?

- Do I just want to have mindless fun for a while?

(That last one is perfectly valid—so long as we know what we're doing, and we consciously choose to do it.)

PURPOSE, ESTEEM, AND MEANINGFUL CONNECTION

Part of mindfulness as it pertains to social media is recognizing and addressing our instinct to use it compulsively. The other side of the equation is choosing to use it consciously to help fulfill all those needs we instinctively want to meet—for others and ourselves.

If social media plays a role in your business, as it does for many of us, your involvement might hinge around various objectives. If you're feeling frustrated with your progress toward your goals, it's tempting to focus on what you lack that other people seem to have, to obsess over followers, engagement, traffic, or any other benchmark. The reality is that numbers don't necessarily measure success, and they're certainly not a requirement for fulfillment.

Some of the most successful people I know have slowly nurtured small, engaged networks of people who provide tremendous value to each other. All of the most fulfilled people I know focus more on the *quality* of their connections than the *quantity* of them. They make it a priority to reveal their authentic self instead of struggling to build and maintain a persona. They take their connections to ever-deepening levels by partnering online, meeting at events offline, and giving those people their full attention when they do connect. And they remember that behind every professional mission, there's a personal purpose.

When we focus on fulfilling our core needs and helping others do the same, we feel more satisfied and, consequently, are more effective. With every meaningful, mutually beneficial engagement, we reinforce our self-esteem, our sense of belonging, and our sense of purpose, enabling more growth and connection. It becomes a self-perpetuating cycle.

In order to do this, you need to challenge the worries that keep you reacting compulsively instead of engaging consciously: the fear that you're missing out on connections or information available somewhere else; the concern that you're not really being heard; or the suspicion that other people are somehow doing better and you're getting left behind.

The reality is that we're all in the same boat. We're all navigating the increasing number of online tools at our disposal, sometimes feeling overwhelmed by the sheer volume of people around us and the barrage of information we need to manage every day. We're all learning how and when to set boundaries, or even take complete breaks to renew and recharge. And we're all discovering that social media provides countless opportunities for personal and professional growth.

Social media can have a profound impact on your life if you let it—but the power of any tool lies in the intentions of its user.

LORI DESCHENE is the founder of tinybuddha.com, a community blog about wisdom that features stories and insights from readers all over the globe. She runs the site as a group effort because she believes we all have something to teach and something to learn. She is also the author of Tiny Buddha: Simple Wisdom for Life's Hard Questions.

→ www.tinybuddha.com

"You can do anything,

but not everything."

— DAVID ALLEN

Q&A:

RECONSIDERING CONSTANT CONNECTIVITY

—

with Tiffany Shlain

As a filmmaker, Tiffany Shlain has been thinking deeply about the impact of technology and connectivity on our culture, our relationships, and our brains for over two decades. A digital pioneer, she founded the Webby Awards and introduced the concept of "cloud filmmaking." While she is the first to appreciate the tremendous power of the web, she is also an advocate of judiciously disconnecting. We spoke with her about the creative benefits of "resetting our brains."

You've said, "We've created a work environment that mirrors our stream of consciousness." Can you explain what you meant?

All of these forms of communication are extensions of us. Going back to [the visionary philosopher of communication theory] Marshall McLuhan: everything is an extension of our desire for connection. We couldn't see far enough, we invented the telescope. We wanted to communicate across distances, we invented the telephone. Then, we wanted to connect with everyone and share all these ideas, and we invented the Internet. We've created this global brain that is very much an extension of our own brains. And because it's an extension of us, it's good and it's bad—because we're both good and bad. We're both focused and distracted. So I think the real problem isn't the technology. I think we need to evolve to know when to turn it off.

You have a regular practice of unplugging called a "technology shabbat." Can you describe what you do?

My husband and I had tried to unplug at various points in our relationship, but we could never quite do it. Then, when my father was dying, I started to think seriously about time and family—how to really be present—and it made me want to take unplugging seriously. So we made a decision as a family that we would do it every week.

We're not super religious, but we are Jewish and we celebrate

Shabbat—the seventh day of the Jewish week, the day of rest. So Friday night we turn off every screen in a very ritualistic way. When we start, we light candles, all the cell phones go off, the TV goes off, and the computers go off. And then we're offline for all of Saturday until after sunset.

Shabbat is a very old idea. If you really look at what some of the scholars from a long time ago wrote about it, it's as though they're talking about today. The idea is that one day a week, you need to get your mind in a different mode, you need to not work. Every week, your brain—and your soul—needs to be reset.

Your soul needs to be reset. That's a great metaphor.

It's like hitting the reset button on my sense of balance. It has just changed my life profoundly. I tell everyone I know to try it. I feel more present with the people I care about, and also more grounded and more creative. Some people say, "Oh, on vacations, I unplug." But when do vacations happen? Once or twice a year. There's something about the weekly practice of getting a different mode of experiencing the world back that's really important.

Do you have other rules about using technology?

Before I started the technology shabbats, my brain was hurting at night. For a while, I was using my cell phone as my alarm clock, but then it was easy to check other things. Now, I don't bring technology into the bedroom. You shouldn't be checking your e-mails before you go to sleep. Your brain gets overstimulated. You need to just unwind your mind.

I'm also a big believer of curating who you follow on social media. You're letting those people into your brain and they're going to influence your thoughts. I find that I even dream about some of the people I follow. We need to be really mindful of who we let into our stream of consciousness.

You've used a Sophocles quote—"Nothing vast enters the life of mortals without a curse"—to talk about the impact of the Internet.

My father [Leonard Shlain] was a writer and he used that quote to describe literacy. But I like to use it to describe the Internet, too. This is a vast, amazing technology that's connecting every mind on the planet, so there's going to be a lot of good, but there are also going to be a lot of things we lose.

That's why all of my projects are really about getting people to stop for a moment in their busy lives and just talk about the curse *and* talk about the good. Because it's a positive and a negative. It feels like there are so many people who think that technology will ruin civilization or who think that it's the best thing in the world. I'm more in the middle. I feel like there are all these great things about it, and there are also some things that I'm worried about. So let's talk about what we're worried about. I believe that once we start having that conversation, it will change the way that we do things.

TIFFANY SHLAIN *is a filmmaker, artist, and founder of the Webby Awards.* Newsweek *called her one of the "Women Shaping the 21st Century." Her last four films premiered at Sundance, including her acclaimed feature documentary,* Connected: An Autoblogography About Love, Death & Technology. *Her book,* Brain Power: From Neurons to Networks, *was published by TED Books.*

→ www.tiffanyshlain.com

"Our intention is to affirm this life, not to bring order out of chaos, nor to suggest improvements in creation...

but simply to wake up to the very life we're living."

— JOHN CAGE

AWAKENING TO
CONSCIOUS COMPUTING

—

Linda Stone

Information overload. Really? Blaming the information doesn't serve us. It's more like information over-consumption. In so many areas of our lives, we've consciously learned to filter. In our digital lives, however, we're still young and inexperienced —particularly with regard to our physical relationship with technology.

Our current relationship with our devices is a dark and twisty tale of chronic stress, the autonomic nervous system, and compromised breathing. But it could be so much better. We're using today's technologies as prosthetics for our minds, when the real opportunity is for these technologies to be prosthetics for our beings.

One of the most significant lifestyle changes to happen over the last twenty years is the increase in the amount of time we each spend in front of one screen or another: television, video games, computers, mobile devices. By some accounts, the average adult spends over eight hours a day in front of a screen.

Survey data collected in 2008 suggested that adults collectively watched 9.8 billion hours of television over the course of a year. In further studies using actuarial tables, researchers determined that, for every hour of television watched by an adult over the age of twenty-five, that adult's life expectancy was reduced by 21.8 minutes. According to a New York Times article reporting on the research, "an adult who spends an average of six hours a day watching TV over the course of a lifetime can expect to live 4.8 years fewer than a person who does not watch TV. These results hold true even for people who exercise regularly."[14]

These researchers tell us that when we're sedentary, our skeletal muscles, especially in our lower limbs, do not contract, thus requiring less fuel. I would further postulate that lymph and blood are more stagnant. Which is why standing and treadmill desks, and looking for opportunities to stand or walk during the course of the day, can contribute to supporting a healthier digital lifestyle.

But the negative impact of sitting is just the tip of the iceberg. Screen time also feeds into a vicious cycle of chronic stress in a way that most of us don't even realize.

THE SURPRISING IMPACT OF SCREEN APNEA

In February 2008, after seven months of research, I wrote about a phenomenon I call e-mail apnea or screen apnea.[15] Screen apnea is the temporary cessation of breath or shallow breathing while sitting in front of a screen, whether a computer, a mobile device, or a television.

To find out how widespread screen apnea was, I observed over two hundred people using computers and smartphones in offices, homes, and cafés. The vast majority of them were holding their breath, or breathing very shallowly, especially when responding to e-mail. What's more, their posture while seated at a computer was often compromised, which only further contributed to restricted breathing.

To explore the impact of this behavior, I called Dr. Margaret Chesney and Dr. David Anderson, then of the National Institutes of Health (NIH). Research conducted by Chesney and Anderson demonstrated that breath-holding contributed significantly to stress-related diseases. The body becomes acidic; the kidneys begin to reabsorb sodium; and the oxygen, carbon dioxide, and nitric oxide balance is undermined, which throws off our biochemistry.

It turns out that nitric oxide, not to be confused with the nitrous oxide used in dental offices, plays an important role in our health. In a briefing document prepared for the Royal Society and Association of British Science Writers, Pearce Wright writes, "The immune system uses nitric oxide in fighting viral, bacterial and parasitic infections, and tumors. Nitric oxide transmits messages between nerve cells and is associated with the processes of learning, memory, sleeping, feeling pain, and, probably, depression."[16] It is also a mediator in inflammation, which is a contributor to obesity.

As I researched the literature and spoke with physicians and researchers about breath-holding, a relationship to the vagus nerve also emerged. The vagus nerve is one of the major cranial nerves, whose primary job is to mediate the autonomic nervous system, which includes the sympathetic ("fight-or-flight") and parasympathetic ("rest-and-digest") nervous systems.

Deep and regular breathing, also referred to as diaphragmatic breathing, helps to quiet the sympathetic nervous system and allows the parasympathetic nervous system—which governs our sense of hunger and satiety, the relaxation response, and many aspects of healthy organ function—to become more dominant.

Conversely, shallow breathing, breath-holding, and hyperventilating trigger the sympathetic nervous system toward a fight-or-flight state. In this state, our heart rate increases, our sense of satiety is compromised, and our bodies gear up for the physical activity that, historically, accompanied a fight-or-flight response. But when the only physical activity is sitting and responding to e-mail, we're sort of "all dressed up with nowhere to go."

Our bodies are tuned to be impulsive and compulsive when we're in fight-or-flight. We also become tuned to over-consume. In this state, we're less aware of when we're hungry and when we're sated. We reach for every available resource, from food to information, as if it's our last opportunity—pulling out our smartphones again and again to check for e-mail, texts, and messages.

Research from the Life and Health Sciences Research Institute in Portugal suggests a possible explanation: sustained stress causes us to fall back on familiar routines. The part of our brain associated with decision-making and goal-directed behaviors shrinks and the brain regions associated with habit formation grow when we're under chronic stress.[17]

WHERE DO WE GO FROM HERE?

Keep in mind: it's not the "what," the technology, that is the core issue here. It's the "how"—how are we using that technology?

A beginning musician is awkward with an instrument and doesn't yet know how to properly breathe, sit, or stand while playing. An experienced musician has learned how to use breath and posture to properly control the instrument. During my investigations in 2008, I noticed that musicians, dancers, athletes, and military test pilots—those who had learned breathing techniques for performance—did not have screen apnea.

Diaphragmatic breathing, Buteyko breathing[1], martial arts, and yoga (pranayama) breathing techniques all have the potential to soothe us, to activate more parasympathetic dominance, and to help our bodies maintain a healthy, regulated autonomic response.

I call the new set of skills we need to learn in order to "embody" when we use technology, Conscious Computing. We need to awaken to the physiology of technology and cultivate a new set of skills related to posture and breathing. In an embodied state, we can reclaim our ability to manage our attention, to think clearly and creatively, and to feel energized and fully engaged.

LINDA STONE is a former senior high-technology executive, and currently a writer, speaker, advisor, and consultant focused on trends and their strategic and consumer implications. She coined the terms continuous partial attention, e-mail apnea, screen apnea, and conscious computing. Her work and articles on her work have appeared in the New York Times, Newsweek, The Economist, The Boston Globe, Harvard Business Review, *and on hundreds of blogs.*

→ www.lindastone.net

---

[1] Buteyko helps people with disordered breathing patterns—such as panic breathing, mouth breathing, or dry coughing to retrain themselves to use a normal breathing pattern at all times. ("What Is Buteyko?" Buteyko Breathing Association, accessed December 17, 2012, http://www.buteykobreathing.org/involve/.)

"Look at the word responsibility — 'RESPONSE-ABILITY'— the ability to choose your response."

— STEPHEN COVEY

RECLAIMING OUR SELF-RESPECT

—

James Victore

Years ago there was a popular book titled *Real Men Don't Eat Quiche*. It billed itself as "A Guidebook to All That Is Truly Masculine." The only advice from the book that I still remember is, "Real men don't have answering machines—if it's important, they'll call back." The book's intent was humor and machismo, but this maxim in particular hints at a level of self-respect that is missing today in our relationship with technology and its tools. We have welcomed technology so fully and lovingly into our lives that we no longer take the time to stop and question the relationship.

Our fun and well-designed portables have got their hooks so deep in us that they are changing our manners and our culture. We no longer see phone calls, IMs, or a "ping" as an intrusion into our personal time and space. The gym and the park are no longer places for personal development or reflection, but just another place to "check in." It used to be that taking a phone call while at the dinner table or on the john was seen as incredibly bad manners or a sign of mental illness. Now it's commonplace and acceptable. Self-respect and etiquette are being nudged out of our lives in lieu of convenient connection. Even work has no time or place and spills out all over our personal lives. We've been sold on the false idea that working from home or, worse, on vacation to help a harried client is a good thing. We are expected to be on call and available to everyone all the time. We've been fitted with an electronic leash for bad bosses, demanding clients, and bored friends.

The crux of this problem is that we are losing the distinction between urgent and important—now everything gets heaped in the urgent pile. And it's quite frankly easier to do the trivial things that are "urgent" than it is to do the important things. But when we choose urgent over important, what we are really choosing is other people's priorities over our own. With every new e-mail, we become like leaves in the wind, reacting to any breeze willy-nilly. We quickly set aside our own concerns to attend to those of others. This busywork pulls our attention from the meaningful work—taking time to think, reflect, and imagine. Yet, it's these pauses that make our lives better and lay the groundwork for our greatest accomplishments.

There are no shortcuts. And any technology-aided shortcut robs you of the work. Recently, a concerned friend of mine suggested an app that could help my meditation practice. I try to be open to new ideas, but this seemed like a choice between playing *Guitar Hero* and actually learning to play guitar. Maybe the work of developing a good meditation practice is worth it. Maybe that's the point. Maybe there are skills I can develop—unaided—that will make me stronger. Why adopt a crutch only to let your muscles atrophy? Why cheat yourself of the effort? The work, the process, *is* the goal. It builds character. It makes us better.

Using technology daily is a relatively new thing. It's omnipresent, dependable ("Can you hear me now?"), and we rely on it more and more. But with new technology comes new habits, and as with any habits—good or bad—we need to be conscientious. Just as we watch our intake of caffeine or candy or alcohol lest we become addicted, we need to consciously develop a healthy relationship with our tools— or we will lose perspective and become slaves to them. As Marshall McLuhan theorized, "We shape our tools, and thereafter our tools shape us." We let our tools take the lead because it's the path of least resistance—the easy way. And the easy way is always a trap.

We have become so trusting of technology that we have lost faith in ourselves and our born instincts. There are still parts of life that we do not need to "better" with technology. It's important to understand that you are smarter than your smartphone. To paraphrase, *there are more things in heaven and earth than are dreamt of in your Google*. Mistakes are a part of life and often the path to profound new insights—so why try to remove them completely? Getting lost while driving or visiting a new city used to be an adventure and a good story. Now we just follow the GPS.

To "know thyself" is hard work. Harder still is to believe that you, with all your flaws, are enough—without checking in, tweeting an update, or sharing a photo as proof of your existence for the approval of your 719 followers. A healthy relationship with your devices is all about taking ownership of your time and making an investment in your life. I'm not calling for any radical, neo-Luddite movement here. Carving out time for yourself is as easy as doing one thing. Walk your dog. Stroll your baby. Go on a date—without your handheld holding your hand. Self-respect, priorities, manners, and good habits are not antiquated ideals to be traded for trends.

Not everyone will be capable of shouldering this task of personal responsibility or of being a good example for their children. But the heroes of the next generation will be those who can calm the buzzing and jigging of outside distraction long enough to listen to the sound of their own hearts, those who will follow their own path until they learn to walk erect—not hunched over like a Neanderthal, palm-gazing. Into traffic.

You have a choice in where to direct your attention. Choose wisely. The world will wait. And if it's important, they'll call back.

JAMES VICTORE is an author, designer, filmmaker, and educator. His work has been exhibited at the Museum of Modern Art in New York and is represented in the permanent collections of museums around the globe. He teaches at the School of Visual Arts in NYC.

→ www.jamesvictore.com

KEY
TAKEAWAYS
–

Taming Your Tools

Get more insights and the desktop wallpaper at:

→ www.99u.com/tools

· KEEP THE LONG VIEW IN VIEW

Post your complex, long-term goals by your workstation to keep them top of mind when prioritizing your tasks.

· BE CONSCIOUS OF YOUR BANDWIDTH

Practice letting go of certain e-mail and social media conversations. There will always be more opportunities than you actually can take on.

· CHECK YOURSELF, OR WRECK YOURSELF

Distinguish between compulsive and conscious behaviors. Are you acting out of boredom or blind habit when you could be serving a higher goal?

· HIT THE RESET BUTTON

Make a ritual of unplugging on a regular basis. Turning everything off is like hitting the "reset" button on your mind—it gives you a fresh start.

· DON'T HOLD YOUR BREATH

Be conscious of your body. Breathing deeply and regularly can decrease your stress levels and help you make better decisions.

· IN IMAGINATION WE TRUST

Don't trust technology over your own instincts and imagination. Doing busywork is easy; doing your best work is hard.

—

CHAPTER FOUR

SHARPENING YOUR CREATIVE MIND

—

How to push through creative blocks and keep the aha moments coming

Bringing incredible creative projects to life demands much hard work down in the trenches of day-to-day idea execution. Genius truly is "1 percent inspiration and 99 percent perspiration."

But we cannot forget the flip side of that 99 percent—it's impossible to solve every problem by sheer force of will. We must also make time for play, relaxation, and exploration, the essential ingredients of the creative insights that help us evolve existing ideas and set new projects in motion.

Often this means creating a routine for breaking from your routine, working on exploratory side projects just for the hell of it, or finding new ways to hotwire your brain's perspective on a problem. It also means learning how to put your inner critic on mute, banish perfectionist tendencies, and push through anxiety-inducing creative blocks.

To stay creatively fit, we must keep our minds engaged and on the move—because the greatest enemy of creativity is nothing more than standing still.

CREATING FOR YOU,
AND YOU ALONE

—

Todd Henry

"When was the last time you made something
that someone wasn't paying you for, and looking
over your shoulder to make sure you got it right?"
When I ask creatives this question, the answer that
comes back all too often is, "I can't remember." It's
so easy for creativity to become a means to a very
practical end—earning a paycheck and pleasing
your client or manager. But that type of work only
uses a small spectrum of your abilities. To truly
excel, you must also continue to create for the most
important audience of all: yourself.

In her book *The Artist's Way*, Julia Cameron discusses a now well-
known practice that she calls "morning pages." She suggests writing

three pages of free-flowing thought first thing in the morning as a way to explore latent ideas, break through the voice of the censor in your head, and get your creative juices flowing. While there is nothing immediately practical or efficient about the exercise, Cameron argues that it's been the key to unlocking brilliant insights for the many people who have adopted it as a ritual.

I've seen similar benefits of this kind of "Unnecessary Creation" in the lives of creative professionals across the board. From gardening to painting with watercolors to chipping away at the next great American novel on your weekends, something about engaging in the creative act on our own terms seems to unleash latent passions and insights.

I believe Unnecessary Creation is essential for anyone who works with his or her mind.

Unnecessary Creation gives you the freedom to explore new possibilities and follow impractical curiosities. Some of the most frustrated creative pros I've encountered are those who expect their day job to allow them to fully express their creativity and satisfy their curiosity. They push against the boundaries set by their manager or client and fret continuously that their best work never finds its way into the end product because of restrictions and compromises. A 2012 survey sponsored by Adobe revealed that nearly 75 percent of workers in the United States, United Kingdom, Germany, France, and Japan felt they weren't living up to their creative potential. (In the United States, the number was closer to 82 percent!)

Obviously, there's a gap between what many creatives actually do each day and what they feel they are capable of doing given more resources or less bureaucracy. But those limitations aren't likely to change in the context of an organization, where there is little tolerance for risk and resources are scarcer than ever. If day-to-day project work is the only work that you are engaging in, it follows that you're going to get frustrated.

To break the cycle, keep a running list of projects you'd like to attempt in your spare time, and set aside a specific time each week (or each day) to make progress on that list. Sometimes this feels very inefficient in the moment, especially when there are so many other urgent priorities screaming for your attention, but it can be a key part of keeping your creative energy flowing for your day-to-day work.

You'll also want to get a notebook to record questions that you'd like to pursue, ideas that you have, or experiments that you'd like to try. Then you can use your pre-defined Unnecessary Creation time to play with these ideas. As Steven Johnson explains in his book *Where Good Ideas Come From*, "A good idea is a network. A specific constellation of neurons—thousands of them—fire in sync with each other for the first time in your brain, and an idea pops into your consciousness. A new idea is a network of cells exploring the adjacent possible of connections that they can make in your mind."[18]

When you give yourself frequent permission to explore the "adjacent possible" with no restrictions on where it leads, you increase the likelihood of a creative breakthrough in all areas of your life and work.

Unnecessary Creation allows you to take risks and develop new skills that can later be applied to your on-demand creating. Have you ever felt like you were in a rut? Perhaps you keep mulling over the same ideas, going to the same wells for inspiration, or opening the same toolbox every time you have to solve a problem. Your tools can become dull and your senses numb when you consistently apply the same old methods. Yet, it's difficult to learn new methods or develop new skills in the midst of your on-demand work because you are being paid to deliver predictable results.

In his book *The Heart Aroused*, the British poet David Whyte writes, "Take any step toward our destiny through creative action (it may be as simple as lifting a pen over a blank sheet of paper), and we know intuitively that we are giving up whatever cover we had."[19] The creative act is inherently risky because it requires you to step out into uncertainty. When you have time scheduled for Unnecessary Creation, you create a safe space to experiment with new ways of working. You get to try and fail without dire consequences. You can create what's in your head rather than adapting what's in your head to someone else's expectations.

These acts of Unnecessary Creation grow your confidence in self-expression, and the skills you develop along the way become new tools in your toolbox that can be applied to your everyday work.

Unnecessary Creation provides a forum for the pursuit of voice, and a reminder that you are not the sum of what you make. You and I are not machines, and no matter how efficient we become at delivering brilliant work, we need regular reminders of our capacity to contribute something unique. We need to stay in touch with the intrinsic desire to strive for the "next" that has driven progress throughout the ages.

The twentieth-century mystic Thomas Merton wrote, "There can be an intense egoism in following everybody else. People are in a hurry to magnify themselves by imitating what is popular—and too lazy to think of anything better. Hurry ruins saints as well as artists. They want quick success, and they are in such a haste to get it that they cannot take time to be true to themselves. And when the madness is upon them, they argue that their very haste is a species of integrity."[20]

Merton elegantly articulates how the pressure of the create-on-demand world can cause us to look sideways at our peers and competitors instead of looking ahead. The process of discovering and refining your voice takes time. Unnecessary Creation grants you the space to discover your unique aptitudes and passions through a process of trial, error, and play that won't often be afforded to you otherwise. Initiating a project with no parameters and no expectations from others also forces you to stay self-aware while learning to listen to and follow your intuition. Both of these are crucial skills for discovering your voice.

It's completely understandable if you're thinking, "But wait—I hardly have time to breathe, and now you want me to cram something else into my schedule, just for my own enjoyment?" It's true that every decision about where we spend our time has an opportunity cost, and dedicating time to Unnecessary Creation seems like a remarkably inefficient choice. In truth, it *is* inefficient.

Consider, however, the opportunity cost of spending your life only on pragmatics. You dedicate your time to pleasing everyone else and delivering on their expectations, but you never get around to discovering your deeper aptitudes and creative capacities. Nothing is worth that.

TODD HENRY *is the founder of Accidental Creative,*
a company that helps creatives and teams be prolific,
brilliant, and healthy. His book, The Accidental
Creative: How to Be Brilliant at a Moment's Notice,
offers strategies for how creative pros can thrive in the
create-on-demand marketplace.

→ www.accidentalcreative.com

"A creator needs only one enthusiast to justify him."

— MAN RAY

TRAINING YOUR MIND TO BE READY FOR INSIGHT

—

Scott McDowell

"Like every beginner, I thought you could beat, pummel, and thrash an idea into existence," Ray Bradbury wrote. "Under such treatment, of course, any decent idea folds up its paws, turns on its back, fixes its eyes on eternity, and dies." So what do you do when you have to be creative and it's just not coming?

Bradbury found a way. "In my early twenties I floundered into a word-association process in which I simply got out of bed each morning, walked to my desk, and put down any word or series of words that happened along in my head."

> *The Lake. The Night. The Crickets. The Ravine. The*
> *Attic. The Basement. The Trapdoor. The Baby. The*
> *Crowd. The Night Train. The Fog Horn. The Scythe. The*
> *Carnival. The Carousel. The Dwarf. The Mirror Maze.*
> *The Skeleton.*

"I would then take arms against the word, or for it, and bring on an assortment of characters to weigh the word and show me its meaning in my own life. An hour or two hours later, to my amazement, a new story would be finished and done."[21]

The most successful creative minds consistently lay the groundwork for ideas to germinate and evolve. They are always refining their personal approach to hijacking the brain's neural pathways, developing a tool kit of tricks to spark the mind like flint on steel.

DISENGAGEMENT, WANDERING, AND REST

When you're working on a sticky problem, the solution is often disengagement. Henry Miller's advice for other writers was to explore unfamiliar sections of the city on bicycle.[22] Composer Steve Reich would ride the subway, another kind of wandering.

Joel Gascoigne, the founder of Buffer, a social media sharing app, cultivates what he calls a "habit of disengagement." In a blog post, "6 Things I Do to Be Consistently Happy," Joel writes, "I go for a walk at 9:30 p.m., along a route which I've done many times before.

Since the route is already decided and is the same every time, I am simply walking and doing nothing else. This prompts reflection and relaxation."

Musician and producer Brian Eno places a high premium on rest, so that new connections can arise:

> *The difficulty of always feeling that you ought to be doing something is that you tend to undervalue the times when you're apparently doing nothing, and those are very important times. It's the equivalent of the dream time, in your daily life, times when things get sorted out and reshuffled. If you're constantly awake work-wise you don't allow that to happen. One of the reasons I have to take distinct breaks when I work is to allow the momentum of a particular direction to run down, so that another one can establish itself.[23]*

Throughout his career, Eno has used a grab bag of approaches to encourage the creative process: intentionally combining disparate ideas, using unfamiliar tools, and developing an elaborate series of creative prompts. "There are lots of ways that you can interfere with it and make it more efficient," says Eno.

LIMITATIONS AND CONSTRAINTS

Sometimes embracing your limitations is the best route forward. George Harrison was staying at Sevenoaks, his parents' bungalow in the English countryside, when he wrote his most enduring Beatles tune:

> I wrote "While My Guitar Gently Weeps" at my mother's house in Warrington. I was thinking about the Chinese I Ching, the Book of Changes...the Eastern concept is that whatever happens is all meant to be, and that there's no such thing as coincidence—every little item that's going down has a purpose. "While My Guitar Gently Weeps" was a simple study based on that theory. I decided to write a song based on the first thing I saw upon opening any book—as it would be relative to that moment, at that time. I picked up a book at random, opened it, saw "gently weeps," then laid the book down again and started the song.[24]

Similarly, many creative directors, designers, and architects often say their best work stems directly from specific client restrictions. Having a set of parameters puts the brain in problem-solving mode; there's something to grip. It may seem counterintuitive, but too big a playing field can muddle the results.

Frank Lloyd Wright insisted that constraints historically have resulted in a flowering of the imagination: "The human race built most nobly when limitations were greatest and, therefore, when most was required of imagination in order to build at all."[25]

Whether or not they're created by an outside client or you yourself, a set of limitations is often the catalyst that sets creativity free.

PHYSICAL POISE AND CALM

What about the body's relationship to creative insight? Anecdotal evidence suggests that monitoring and replenishing your energy may well lead to greater creative output. Many of our brightest minds have used some combination of daily spiritual or physical preparation. Photographer William Wegman rides his bike as many as twenty miles a day while National Book Award winner John Irving still trains like a wrestler at age seventy.

Exercise sharpens brain activity, reports *Newsweek*: "Almost every dimension of cognition improves from thirty minutes of aerobic exercise, and creativity is no exception. The type of exercise doesn't matter, and the boost lasts for at least two hours afterward."[26]

Regular sleep doesn't hurt, either. According to a Harvard study, with proper sleep and incubation, "People are 33 percent more likely to infer connections among distantly related ideas."[27]

A daily meditation practice is another kind of preparation. Oscar-winning actor Jeff Bridges and Grammy-winning musician Moby both meditate regularly. At its best, meditation trains your mind to be attentive and focused, and it's commonly assumed to reduce stress. Over time, meditation can lead to better use of the brain's faculties, a greater sense of compassion, and increased sensitivity to the inherent connections between ideas.

In his book *Catching the Big Fish*, filmmaker David Lynch suggests that companies can solve productivity problems by advocating meditation:

> *Instead of instilling fear, if a company offered a way for everyone in the business to dive within—to start expanding energy and intelligence—people would work overtime for free. They would be far more creative. And the company would just leap forward. This is the way it can be. It's not the way it is, but it could be that way so easily.*[28]

Ultimately, there's no definitive way to manufacture insight. It's situational, and it comes down to what works for you. What we do know for sure is that whenever your brain senses a pattern and gets too comfortable, creativity stagnates and it's time to try something else.

In the end, preparing for insight is all about being persistent, throwing a wrench into the works from time to time, and always working to stay one step ahead of complacency.

SCOTT MCDOWELL *works with nonprofit and socially-minded business leaders to solve big problems and generate organizational potency. He runs the consulting and executive search firm CHM Partners. Andy Warhol was right: "Making money is art and working is art and good business is the best art." Scott once produced MTV's 120 Minutes and currently hosts* The Long Rally *on WFMU.*

→ www.chm-partners.com

"Your mind will answer most questions if you learn to relax and wait for the answer."

— WILLIAM S. BURROUGHS

Q&A:

TRICKING YOUR BRAIN INTO CREATIVITY

—

with Stefan Sagmeister

Designer and typographer Stefan Sagmeister is known for his unorthodox approach to creativity. Whether it's writing a message on the ground of a public square using 250,000 coins or taking a year-long sabbatical every seven years, Sagmeister brings a unique level of meticulous craft and thoughtfulness to his work. As evidenced by his book *Things I Have Learned in My Life So Far*, he's also partial to extracting lessons from his life experience. We spoke with him about how brain hacks can lead us to aha moments and why nothing is more important than mapping big creative projects right into your daily schedule.

You have to produce great creative work on a daily basis. Do you have any rituals for finding a rhythm?

I try to do the most difficult things early in the morning. If I start with easy stuff, meaning if I start checking and answering e-mail, it's very difficult to then convince myself to do difficult things later on.

What do you do when you need a breakthrough?

One trick I use a lot is to think about a problem from a totally different point of view. It's a technique from Edward de Bono, a philosopher from Malta. He wrote a number of books about the nature of thinking and how to get better at it.

The idea is that you take a starting point that has nothing to do with the project itself. I used this technique for the identity we did for a music center in Portugal—Casa da Musica. It came out of the point of view of a car. I was looking out from a terrace, and I saw a car, and then I started thinking about the identity from the perspective of a car. Let's see, it's moving. It's moving, oh, maybe it goes from one thing to another. The perspective needs to change the identity, and so forth. In the end, of course, nobody could tell that the Casa da Musica identity came from cars.

The reason that de Bono thinks this works is because our brain is so incredibly good at thinking in repetition. If you want to come up with a new idea, the first thing you can always do is think of something that you did before or something that you've seen before. So starting with someone, or somewhere, else is just basically a trick to fool the brain out of thinking in repetition.

What about creative constraints? Do you think they can help?

I think that any kind of limitation is useful. Any kind of limitation that is clear, and that's there from the beginning. Brian Eno has this wonderful little quote about the electric guitar. He says the electric guitar became the dominant instrument of the twentieth century simply because it's such a stupid instrument. It can do so very little. But it can do a few things very, very well, and therefore it allows human nature to go to the edge of what's possible.

You're making a documentary called The Happy Film. Do you find that exploring another medium like film feeds back into your design process in useful ways?

I feel the most satisfied if I work on projects where I know about half of what I'm doing and I don't know the other half. If I go too much in one direction, meaning if I know too little about something, I get too anxious. And if I know too much about something, I get too bored.

How do you find time to work on the film amid all of your client projects?

I have Friday set aside as a film day. But the work was quite difficult to keep up in the beginning of the film, because there wasn't any real structure and there was no forward momentum besides me thinking about it. Now it has become easier because there are other people involved, and there are things that need to be done—whether I feel like doing them or not.

When you were working on your own, how did you stay motivated?

Well, I know from my sabbaticals that I have to carve out time and that time has to stay untouched no matter what. Okay, I'm gonna do Friday film day. So I went to the calendar and I crossed out all Fridays and every single day had a film day in there. So when I have to schedule something four months in advance and somebody wants to meet me on a Friday, I can say, "No, I can't meet you on a Friday, you can meet me on a Thursday." Now, I think that's pretty much Planning 101. You put the things that you really want do into your calendar.

There's a wonderful story about a Nobel Prize winner…He was asked by some corporation to talk about time planning. He gets up in front of the group with a glass jar, and he says, "All I can tell you about time planning, I can show you in two minutes." Then he takes out a bunch of big stones and puts them into the jar, filling it up to the top, then he takes out a pocketful of tiny stones and puts them in, then he pours some sand in, and then finally he pours some water into the jar—and that's how it all fits.

The moral was pretty clear, we have to put the big stones in first; otherwise, the other stuff won't fit.

So the big stones are our big creative projects in this case?

Exactly, the stuff you really want to do. If you don't put those things into your calendar and stand by that time, it's never going to get done. All the small stuff will trickle in and there won't be room.

If you want do projects that you really love, you have to be aware of how difficult they are to do. For a long time I wasn't doing certain projects, but I thought I would love to do them if I had the time. Then, when I had the time, I avoided doing them because of all the other stuff that I still needed to do, like e-mail. And it's just so much easier to do e-mail than to actually sit down and think.

I think we need that self-awareness. That we don't have time because it's convenient not to have the time, because maybe we don't want to challenge ourselves.

STEFAN SAGMEISTER *is a New York–based graphic designer and typographer who operates the design firm Sagmeister & Walsh Inc. He has designed album covers for Lou Reed, OK Go, The Rolling Stones, David Byrne, Aerosmith, and Pat Metheny, and he is the author of* Things I Have Learned in My Life So Far.

→ www.sagmeister.com

"The artist who aims at perfection in everything achieves it in nothing."

— EUGENE DELACROIX

LETTING GO OF PERFECTIONISM

—

Elizabeth Grace Saunders

"I can't be a perfectionist because nothing I do is ever perfect," was my not-so-self-aware response when one of my mentors suggested that I might have perfectionist tendencies. In the seven years since I received that feedback—and came to understand she had in fact diagnosed me perfectly—I've grappled with how to manage these "tendencies" so that they don't undermine my ability to produce great work.

I've discovered that, regardless of our patterns of behavior in the past, we can choose to act differently in the present—and that a conscious decision to not let perfectionism control us makes a huge difference in our ability to break through our limits and enjoy the creative process.

In case you're wondering if you suffer from the same ailment that plagued me for decades, here are a few definitions of perfectionism:

> *A personality disposition characterized by an individual striving for flawlessness and setting excessively high performance standards, accompanied by overly critical self-evaluations and concerns regarding others' evaluations.*[29]
>
> *A disposition to regard anything short of perfection as unacceptable.*[30]

Do either of these sound strangely familiar?

These definitions highlight the two primary mental patterns, idealism and judgment, that lead to the two central emotional states, fear and pride. From a perfectionist's point of view, if you manage to force yourself into producing at the level you envisioned in your head, you feel on top of the world. If you can't measure up to those standards, you're crushed.

Admittedly, this striving can lead to some pretty incredible work. Artists, writers, and designers have produced breathtakingly executed pieces due to their relentless pursuit of the ideal. But at what cost?

An overemphasis on perfection can lead to enormous stress

(think angry flare-ups or spontaneous tears). At best, it can make you hesitate to immerse yourself in a new project. At worst, this pattern can lead to you abandoning your creative pursuits because of the toll they take on you physically, mentally, and emotionally.

Ironically, perfectionism can also inhibit your ability to reach your full potential. If you refuse to put yourself in a situation where you might give an imperfect performance, you'll prevent yourself from receiving the proper feedback, input, and direction necessary for additional growth.

To help you achieve breakthroughs in areas where perfectionism may be holding you back, I've outlined two contrasting approaches that you can take at each phase of the creative process. The creative perfectionist approach can help you identify if perfectionism stands in the way of your progress. The creative pragmatist approach demonstrates a more effective way to proceed.

In all cases, you are the "I," your important creative work is the "piece," and the ability to decide how you move forward lies within your control. Choose wisely.

STUCK AT THE START

The Creative Perfectionist Approach: I cannot start my new piece until the ideal moment, meaning I have a large uninterrupted block of time, no other distractions, a strong level of motivation to work on the project, and the ideal plan for how to optimize the entire process. This typically means that I end up doing nothing—and feeling horribly guilty about procrastinating—until I have no other choice but to begin. This forces me to proceed at a frantic pace, staying up all hours of the night and neglecting almost everything else. I'm so frustrated because I know I could do a better job if I had just started sooner.

The Creative Pragmatist Approach: I know there will never be an ideal time to begin so I set aside time to get started on one part of the process. When I get to that time, regardless of whether I feel like doing the work or whether it seems like the most urgent priority at the moment, I get started on what I can do now. At the end of that initial start, I decide when I will move forward on the project again. I understand that the first stage of working on the piece is messy and that the project inevitably will take longer and have more complexity than I initially anticipate. But that's okay because I have time to adapt and adjust my plans and still meet my goals and create good work.

LOST IN THE MIDDLE

The Creative Perfectionist Approach: I must obsess over every detail of the piece, regardless of whether anyone else will notice. This leads me to revise and edit myself at every step instead of giving myself permission to bang out an imperfect first draft. Also, whenever I think of something I could research in relation to my piece, I delve into learning as much as possible about the subject, even if I do not really need the information and could never use all of it. This leads to my spending lots and lots of time on my piece but not having much in the way of tangible results to show for my efforts. I also end up feeling really overwhelmed because I know so much that it makes it difficult to focus and narrow down my possibilities. This means that I often overdo the first part of my creative project in terms of time spent and attention to detail. Then I can barely skim the surface of what I should do for the rest of the piece when it comes close to crunch time.

The Creative Pragmatist Approach: I define the meaningful end deliverables and then start to clarify the intermediate steps to create them. I look at how much time I have between now and my projected end date. By "time" I mean both number of weeks and number of hours during those weeks to move this project forward. Then I allocate my time budget to the incremental steps, weighted by the reality of the minimum time that it takes to complete the elements and also by the importance of that element to the overall success of the project.

Then, as I move through the process, I push myself to keep pace with the goals I've set, producing good enough work within the time I have to spend and giving myself permission to circle back if I still have additional hours at the end. This will ensure that I don't over-invest in less important items and then botch the finish.

REFUSAL TO FINISH

The Creative Perfectionist Approach: If I can think of anything more that I could possibly do to improve, refine, or add to the piece, then it isn't done. If the work hasn't attained the ideal set in my head at the start, it's inaccurate to say it's complete.

The Creative Pragmatist Approach: I define "finished" as having at least met the minimum requirements for the piece and as knowing that I've done the best I could given the time and resources allocated to the project. Saying something is complete doesn't mean that it can't be improved upon or elaborated on in the future. It just means that I can submit it and move on to other work.

DREAD OF FEEDBACK

The Creative Perfectionist Approach: If someone points out a mistake, has a different opinion, mentions something I didn't include, or has anything other than incredibly positive things to say about a piece, I feel embarrassed and like a total failure. I worry that my expertise and respect is in question and that others will think I'm incompetent and an impostor.

The Creative Pragmatist Approach: I appreciate feedback because it helps me to test and refine my work. I may agree or disagree with the input and I can choose how I respond to it. If I never open myself up to others' insights, I might miss out on something really wonderful. My work is improved and my world is expanded through the input of others.

A FINAL NOTE ON LETTING GO

As a recovering perfectionist myself, I completely understand that what I have described as the Creative Pragmatist Approach may sound like (gasp!) settling. To a perfectionist, settling seems worse than not completing the piece, which is why perfectionists often produce very little. But I really want to challenge you to look through these examples again and test them out in your creative process. My guess is that you'll find you produce far more and far better work with much less stress by aiming for less-than-perfect. This approach allows you to recapture the energy that you typically waste on emotional angst so that you can focus it on the elements of the creative process that matter most.

ELIZABETH GRACE SAUNDERS *is the author of* The 3 Secrets to Effective Time Investment: How to Achieve More Success with Less Stress *and the founder and CEO of Real Life E Time Coaching & Training. Elizabeth is dedicated to empowering people around the world to accomplish more with peace and confidence.*

→ www.ScheduleMakeover.com

"Creativity is not a talent.

It is a way of operating."

— JOHN CLEESE

GETTING UNSTUCK

—

Mark McGuinness

Novelist Vikram Seth once found himself blocked after writing the first hundred pages of a story set in post-independence India. In spite of his best efforts to move the story forward, it stubbornly resisted, until one day he realized he had overlooked the real problem: he simply didn't know enough about the period.

Once he understood this, Seth switched from writing to research, reading old newspapers, visiting key places, and interviewing people who had lived through the era. This gave him so much material that his planned short novel grew into a 1,500-page doorstop. The finished work, *A Suitable Boy*, landed him a rumored $1.1 million advance and established him as a literary superstar.[31]

I find this story encouraging for two reasons: first, if you're wrestling with a creative block, it's a great reminder that even the stars get stuck; second, it shows that the solution can be surprisingly straightforward once you understand the problem correctly.

Faced with a block, it would have been easy for Seth to question his abilities or to keep banging his head against it. But it turned out that there was nothing wrong with his literary talents, and trying harder at the wrong thing wasn't getting him anywhere. He simply didn't know enough, so he needed to learn more. Once he did that, the story started to flow again.

The next time you experience a creative block, resist the temptation to doubt yourself, or to put in more blind effort. Stop and ask yourself what *kind* of block you are experiencing. Once you're clear about the nature of the problem, it will be easier to solve it. To help you get started, here are six of the most common types of creative block, with solutions for each.

INSPIRATION DROUGHT

When working on a large creative project, you may reach a point where your initial inspiration runs dry. You find it harder and harder to muster any enthusiasm for the work, let alone original ideas.

The Adventures of Tom Sawyer is regarded as one of the great American novels, but at one point its author despaired of finishing it. In his *Autobiography*, Mark Twain describes reaching a point in the story where he felt unable to go on: "My tank had run dry." He abandoned it for two years and turned his mind to other things. When he eventually picked up the manuscript again, he made the "great discovery" that the "tank" of his imagination had refilled itself in the meantime, and he was able to complete the story. This discovery was a turning point in Twain's writing career: he learned to watch out for the point in each subsequent book when his tank ran dry, and to take a break before finishing it.

Take a leaf out of Twain's book. Look out for the telltale signs that your tank is empty, and use them as a cue to take a break and let your unconscious take the strain. Relax or apply yourself to a completely different type of project. You may not have two years to set your project aside if a deadline is looming, but even a short break can work wonders when you're running low on inspiration.

EMOTIONAL BARRIER

Creativity can be intense. Faced with the unknown, you may be scared of what you'll discover or reveal about yourself. Maybe your subject matter is painful, embarrassing, or downright weird. Whatever you're trying to avoid, the only end product is procrastination.

When I was a student, the novelist John Fowles spoke at my college. When somebody asked if he had any advice for young writers, he talked about feeling embarrassed about the sexual content of some of his novels when he imagined his parents reading them. In the end he burst through the barrier by mentally shouting, "Fuck my parents!" as he sat down to write.

Give yourself permission to write, draw, or otherwise express whatever comes out—on the understanding that you will not make it public, at least for a while. Privacy will make it easier to get the draft version done. Then take a break before deciding whether you want to show it to an audience.

MIXED MOTIVATIONS

There's quite a bit of evidence that extrinsic motivations—such as money and reputation—have a negative impact on creativity. It's only when you're focused on intrinsic motivations—such as your fascination with the material or the sheer pleasure you take in creating it—that you do your best work.

This explains the well-known phenomenon of "sophomore slumps" among bands. When let loose in the studio for their first album, the musicians can barely contain their enthusiasm over being given the opportunity to make their music the way they had always wanted to. But if the album brings success, it also brings pressure—there's more riding on the follow-up, they have a reputation and lifestyle to maintain—which makes them more likely to start second-guessing their instincts.

Once the contract is signed and the deal is done (whether it's an album, client commission, or a job), put all thoughts of rewards out of your mind and focus relentlessly on the work itself. It may help to have a studio or other space dedicated to creative work—a place you never "contaminate" by talking business or daydreaming about success while you're there.

PERSONAL PROBLEMS

Creativity demands focus, and it's hard to concentrate if you're getting divorced, dealing with a teething toddler, battling an addiction, falling out with your best friend, grieving someone special, moving houses, or locked in a dispute with a neighbor. If you're lucky, you'll only have to deal with these kinds of things one at a time—but troubles often come in twos or threes.

Frida Kahlo's life was marked by suffering. She had polio as a child followed by a terrible traffic accident as teenager, which led to chronic health issues. She spent long periods alone and in pain. Her stormy marriage—then divorce and remarriage—to fellow Mexican painter Diego Rivera brought a whole new set of problems, including infidelities and professional rivalry. Kahlo turned to painting when she was bedridden after her accident, and her dedication to her art was a constant throughout the tribulations of her personal life. She transformed her solitary suffering into art: "I paint myself because I am so often alone and because I am the subject I know best."

Treat your work as a refuge—an oasis of control and creative satisfaction in the midst of the bad stuff. Don't beat yourself up if you're not on fire creatively every day—give yourself credit if you show up for work and make even a small amount of progress. When you put down your tools for the day, you may even see your personal situation with a fresh eye.

POVERTY

This isn't just about money, although a lack of cash is a perennial problem for creatives. You could also be time-poor, knowledge-poor, have a threadbare network, or be short of equipment or other things you need to get the job done.

Samuel Johnson famously wrote his book *Rasselas* in one week to cover his mother's funeral expenses. Shane Carruth wrote, directed, produced, and starred in his cult movie *Primer*, filming it in five weeks and keeping the cost down to $7,000 by filling the cast with friends and family and doing everything himself. In order to capitalize on the chart success of their singles, the Beatles recorded ten songs in a single day at a reported £400 to complete their debut album, *Please Please Me*.

Make a virtue of necessity and set yourself the creative challenge of achieving as much as possible with what you have. If you're still in doubt, consider the first and second *Star Wars* trilogies and ask yourself whether more resources always equal better results.

PRESENTATION PROBLEMS

In 1976, Iggy Pop's career was on the skids. His band, the Stooges, had disintegrated in chaos and his drug use had gotten so out of control that he checked himself into a psychiatric hospital. Afterward, his friend David Bowie invited him to travel as a guest on the *Station to Station* tour; Pop was impressed by the smooth operation of Bowie's touring and marketing machine. The following year Bowie produced Pop's albums *The Idiot* and *Lust for Life* and toured with him to promote them. They became his best-known solo releases. Bowie had always admired Pop's talents as a writer and performer, but it took a production and marketing makeover before the wider world sat up and took notice.

If you've spent years plugging away with a minuscule audience or client list, you may start to wonder why you bother. You may not see yourself as a natural marketer, but sometimes a few tweaks to your presentation can make a huge difference to your impact and the rewards you reap. Which in turn can replenish your enthusiasm for your work.

This is where creativity blends into communication skills. You need to understand and influence the right people. Which means beefing up your presentation, marketing, and networking skills. It doesn't matter if you're shy or introverted. If you want to succeed, you need to communicate. And grow a thicker skin. Show me a creative who's never suffered a setback or a bad review, and you won't be pointing at a superstar.

～ⅅⅅ～

Mann, Fowles, Kahlo, Twain, Pop...if you're feeling stuck and discouraged, take heart from the fact that you're in good company. None of these "greats" were immune from creative blocks. In fact, one of the things that made them great was their persistence in the face of self-doubt, criticism, and rejection.

I'm not saying you should seek these things out, but don't shy away from them either. If you accept that they are simply an occupational hazard for creative professionals, you've taken the first step toward getting unstuck and back in your creative zone.

MARK MCGUINNESS *is a coach for creative professionals. Based in London, he coaches clients all over the world and consults for creative companies. He is the author of the book* Resilience: Facing Down Rejection and Criticism on the Road to Success *and a columnist for 99U.*

→ www.LateralAction.com

KEY
TAKEAWAYS

—

Sharpening Your Creative Mind

- **PRACTICE UNNECESSARY CREATION**
  Use personal creative projects to explore new obsessions, skills, or ways of working in a low-pressure environment.

- **WANDER LONELY AS A CLOUD**
  Make time for your mind—and body—to wander when you're stuck. Disengaging from the problem allows your subconscious to do its work.

- **DEFINE "FINISHED" FROM THE START**
  Keep your inner perfectionist in check by defining what finished looks like at the beginning of a project. And when you get there, stop!

- **DON'T GO ON AUTOPILOT**
  Repetition is the enemy of insight. Take unorthodox—even wacky—approaches to solving your stickiest problems and see what happens.

- **SEARCH FOR THE SOURCE**
  When the well runs dry, don't blame a lack of talent. Creative blocks frequently piggyback on other problems. See if you can identify them.

- **LOVE YOUR LIMITATIONS**
  Look at constraints as a benefit, rather than an impediment. They activate our creative thinking by upping the ante.

A CALL

TO

ACTION

—

A parting message on taking it to the next level

HOW PRO CAN YOU GO?

—

by Steven Pressfield

In our youth, when we're operating as amateurs, we're no use to ourselves or to anyone else—at least in the realm of fulfilling our destiny, the arena of getting something done.

At the amateur level, the only skills we possess are those of dropping the ball, flaking out, panicking at opportunities, over-aggressively asserting our "rights," and in general getting in our own way.

When we turn pro, all that changes.

But turning pro is not a one-and-done proposition. There are many levels of professionalism. It's important, I believe, to have a concept of these levels from the start. The long view. What are we getting ourselves into when we say, "I want to paint," "I want to launch a start-up," "I want to shoot film"?

Here's my version of the road map, as these steps have unfolded in my own life. Stage One is simply being able to sit down and work, if only for a single hour. Don't laugh. Ninety-nine out of a hundred can't do it. This stage is entry-level. It's kindergarten. Still, I confess it took me seven years of hell to reach this stage, one night in a Manhattan sublet many moons ago.

The next stage is being able to repeat that single hour. Can we work again the next day? Can we stay at it all day? Can we keep it up for a week?

At this stage we are like the cartoon fish emerging from the primeval sea to take its first halting flipper-steps onto dry land. This moment is huge. It's epochal. But we're still just a Cambrian coelacanth crawling at .0001 miles per hour and gasping for oxygen with our gills.

(At this stage, by the way, we're not even thinking about quality. The idea that you and I might eventually produce something—a book, a film, a start-up—worthy of the attention of another human being... that's so far off, we can't even conceive of it.)

What we're doing in fact is learning (teaching ourselves, because they don't have courses in this stuff at the Wharton School or the

Iowa Writers' Workshop) how to manage our emotions, control our impulse to self-sabotage, and keep on truckin' in the face of adversity.

Stage Three is Crossing the Finish Line. Starting at "A" is easy. But can we make it all the way to "Z"? Can we type THE END and actually have something in between that stands up?

(From my own initial moment of turning pro, it took another four years to reach this point.)

If we can write a chapter, can we write a short story? If we can film a short subject, can we put together a feature?

At this stage, we are no longer breathing through gills. We have lungs now; we are standing on our hind legs and speaking in complete sentences. And we're beginning to address quality. We're acquiring craft, experience, and skill. We have produced a product that works, that delivers value for others, and that stands on its own in the marketplace. Are we pros yet?

Yes and no.

We have banged out one work, but can we deliver two?

I define Resistance as that self-created and self-perpetuated, invisible, impersonal, indefatigable force whose sole aim is to prevent us from doing our work, from becoming our best selves, and from rising to the next level of competence, integrity, and generosity.

That force never goes away. In fact, it becomes more protean and more cunning as we advance through the levels of professionalism.

It will try to kill us now between Work #1 and Work #2. It will attack us by making us arrogant. We will become self-inflated, complacent. At the same time, Resistance will undermine us with fear. It will tell us we're a One-Hit Wonder, a flash in the pan.

The passage from Success #1 to Success #2 is another epochal odyssey. It's our Hero's Journey. Within this ordeal, we acquire simultaneously self-reliance and self-surrender.

We're talking, now, about a career.

If you're a writer, can you picture a shelf of books with your name on the spines? If you're a moviemaker, can you envision your filmography on IMDb? If you're an entrepreneur, can you evolve and reinvent yourself through Start-up #1 to Failure #6, from Crash-and-Burn #9 to Blockbuster #12 and beyond?

Can you handle success? Can you resurrect yourself after failure? Can you delegate? Can you outsource? Can you work with others? Can you turn around and help the next generation coming up behind you?

Will your ethics fail under pressure? Will you pander, will you sell out? What about when the world changes and books/movies/

philanthropic ventures are all being produced by robots? Can you relocate to Mars and start again?

As you travel through life, let this be our goal: keep your eye on the donut and not on the hole.

But what is the donut?

Is it money? Power, sex, glory, notoriety? Is it service? Altruism? Do we really have a "message" we want to send?

What is a professional, anyway?

A professional is someone who can keep working at a high level of effort and ethics, no matter what is going on—for good or ill—around him or inside him.

A professional shows up every day.

A professional plays hurt.

A professional takes neither success nor failure personally.

In the end, for me, it comes down to the work itself. A pro gets younger and more innocent as he or she ascends through the levels. It's a paradox. We get salty and cynical, but we creep closer, too, to the wonder. You have to or you can't keep going. Any other motivation will burn you out.

You develop a practice, and the practice gets simpler and less self-oriented over time. We rise through the levels of professionalism by a process of surrender. We surrender to our gift, whatever that may be. We give ourselves up to the goddess and to the process.

As Shakespeare or Sappho or Bruce Springsteen evolve from work to work, yet always retain their Shakespeare-ness, Sappho-ness, and Springsteenitude, so, too, you and I must keep morphing to the melody that our ears alone can hear. Each level gets harder, each threshold demands more.

Is this a path you want to travel? Did someone say it was easy? Do you have a choice?

STEVEN PRESSFIELD *is the author of* The War of Art *and* Turning Pro *and the novels* Gates of Fire, The Legend of Bagger Vance *and* The Profession.

→ www.stevenpressfield.com

"Inspiration is for amateurs, the rest of us just show up and get to work."

— CHUCK CLOSE

ACKNOWLEDGEMENTS

—

Much applause must go to our incredible brain trust of contributors: Dan Ariely, Leo Babauta, Scott Belsky, Lori Deschene, Aaron Dignan, Erin Rooney Doland, Seth Godin, Todd Henry, Christian Jarrett, Scott McDowell, Mark McGuinness, Cal Newport, Steven Pressfield, Gretchen Rubin, Stefan Sagmeister, Elizabeth Grace Saunders, Tony Schwartz, Tiffany Shlain, Linda Stone, and James Victore. This book would quite literally be nothing without your insights and expertise. Thank you for the time, energy, and generosity it took to share them with us.

I owe many thanks for the beautiful cover designs and interior layout to the vision of Behance co-founder and chief of design Matias Corea—one of my absolute favorite creative collaborators— and to the excellent eye of our talented designer Raewyn Brandon.

This book would not exist, nor would it read so effortlessly, without the enthusiasm, advocacy, and editorial chops of David Moldawer at Amazon, who has been a stalwart supporter of Behance and 99U since the early days. Thank you for believing in our mission and helping us bring it to a larger audience.

I am also indebted to Courtney Dodson for shepherding this book gracefully through production, to 99U associate editor Sean Blanda for incisive thoughts on the manuscript, and to the entire Behance and Amazon teams for their incredible support, talent, and tenacity.

Lastly, I must extend much, much appreciation to Scott Belsky for his invaluable input on planning, shaping, and refining this book series, and—more important—for believing in me. Having the chance to lead 99U as part of Behance's mission to empower the creative world has been—and will continue to be—an incredible and invigorating opportunity for which I am deeply grateful.

ABOUT 99U

—

99U is Behance's effort to deliver the "missing curriculum" that you didn't get in school, highlighting best practices for making ideas happen. We do this through interviews, articles, and videos on our Webby Award–winning website at 99u.com, our annual 99 Conference in New York City, our bestselling book *Making Ideas Happen,* and our ongoing 99U book series, of which *Manage Your Day-to-Day* is the first installment.

→ *www.99u.com*

ABOUT THE EDITOR

—

As editor-in-chief and director, Jocelyn K. Glei leads the 99U in its mission to provide the "missing curriculum" on making ideas happen. She oversees the 99u.com website—which has won two Webby Awards for "Best Cultural Blog"—and leads the curation and execution of the popular 99 Conference, which has presented talks from visionary creatives including Jack Dorsey, Beth Comstock, John Maeda, Jonathan Adler, Stefan Sagmeister, Jad Abumrad, and many more.

Prior to joining Behance and 99U, Jocelyn was the global managing editor at the online media company Flavorpill, leading development of new editorial products. She has also consulted with dozens of brands and agencies, from Herman Miller to PSFK to Huge Inc, on content strategy and web launches. She loves creating content-driven products that people love.

→ *www.jkglei.com*

END NOTES

—

1. Lisa Rogak, *Haunted Heart: The Life and Times of Stephen King* (New York: Thomas Dunne Books, 2009), 93.

2. Ben Yagoda, "Slow Down, Sign Off, Tune Out," *New York Times*, October 22, 2009.

3. L. L. Bowman et al., "Can Students Really Multitask? An Experimental Study Of Instant Messaging While Reading," *Computers and Education*, 54 (2010): 927–931.

4. S. T. Iqbal and E. Horvitz, "Disruption and Recovery of Computing Tasks: Field Study, Analysis, and Directions," Proceedings of the Conference on Human Factors in Computing Systems, 2007.

5. A. Bucciol, D. Houser and M. Piovesan. "Temptation At Work," Harvard Business School Research Paper, no. 11-090, 2011.

6. S. Leroy, "Why Is It So Hard To Do My Work? The Challenge Of Attention Residue When Switching Between Work Tasks," *Organizational Behavior and Human Decision Processes*, 109, no. 2 (2009): 168–181.

7. Walter Mischel, Ebbe B. Ebbesen, and Antonette Raskoff Zeiss, "Cognitive And Attentional Mechanisms In Delay Of Gratification," *Journal of Personality and Social Psychology*, vol. 21, no. 2 (1972): 204–218.

8. R. Baumeister and J. Tierney, *Willpower: Rediscovering the Greatest Human Strength.* (New York: Penguin Press, 2011).

9. Kimberly D. Elsbach and Andrew B. Hargadon, "Enhancing Creativity Through 'Mindless' Work: A Framework of Workday Design," *Organization Science*, 17 (4) 470–483.

10. Murakami Haruki, *What I Talk About When I Talk About Running* (New York: Vintage, 2009).

11. Chip Bayers, "The Inner Bezos." *WIRED*, March 1999.

12. Michael Chui et al., "The Social Economy: Unlocking Value And Productivity Through Social Technologies," McKinsey Global Institute, 2012.

13. Diana I. Tamir and Jason P. Mitchell, "Disclosing Information About The Self Is Intrinsically Rewarding," *PNAS*, vol. 109, no. 21(2012): 8038–8043.

14. Gretchen Reynolds, "Get Up. Get Out. Don't Sit," *New York Times*, October 17, 2012.

15. Linda Stone, "Just Breathe: Building the Case for E-mail Apnea," *Huffington Post*, February 8, 2008.

16. Pearce Wright, "Nitric Oxide: From Menace To Marvel Of The Decade." A briefing document prepared for the Royal Society and Association of British Science Writers, 1997.

17. Natalie Angier, "Brain Is a Co-Conspirator in a Vicious Stress Loop," *New York Times*, August 17, 2009.

18. Steven Johnson, *Where Good Ideas Come From: The Natural History of Innovation* (New York: Riverhead Books, 2011), 45.

19. David Whyte, *The Heart Aroused: Poetry and the Preservation of the Soul in Corporate America* (New York: Crown Business, 1996), 83.

20. Thomas Merton and Sue Monk Kidd, *New Seeds of Contemplation* (New York: New Directions, 2007), 98.

21. Ray Bradbury, *Zen in the Art of Writing* (Santa Barbara, CA: Capra Press, 1989).

22. Henry Miller, *On Writing* (New York: New Directions, 1964).

23. Eric Tamm, *Brian Eno: His Music and the Vertical Color of Sound* (New York: Da Capo, 1995).

24. Beatles, *The Beatles Anthology.* (San Francisco: Chronicle Books, 2000).

25. Frank Lloyd Wright, *The Essential Frank Lloyd Wright: Critical Writings on Architecture* (Princeton, NJ: Princeton University Press, 2008).

26. Po Bronson and Ashley Merryman, "The Creativity Crisis," *Newsweek*, July 10, 2010.

27. Leslie Berlin, "We'll Fill This Space, but First a Nap," *New York Times*, September 27, 2008.

28. David Lynch, *Catching the Big Fish: Meditation, Consciousness, and Creativity* (New York: Tarcher, 2007), 74.

29. Wikipedia contributors, "Perfectionism (psychology)," Wikipedia, The Free Encyclopedia, accessed November 16, 2012, http://en.wikipedia.org/wiki/Perfectionism_(psychology).

30. "perfectionism," *Merriam-Webster.com*, accessed November 16, 2012, http://www.merriam-webster.com/dictionary/perfectionism.

31. Richard B. Woodward, "Vikram Seth's Big Book," *New York Times*, May 2, 1993.

INDEX

—